IE Business Publishing

IE Business Publishing and Palgrave Macmillan have launched a collection of high-quality books in the areas of Business and Management, Economics and Finance. This important series is characterized by innovative ideas and theories, entrepreneurial perspectives, academic rigor and practical approaches which will make these books invaluable to the business professional, scholar and student alike.

IE Business School is one of the world's leading institutions dedicated to educating business leaders. Palgrave Macmillan, part of Macmillan Group, has been serving the learning and professional sector for more than 160 years.

The series, put together by these eminent international partners, will enable executives, students, management scholars and professionals worldwide to have access to the most valuable information and critical new arguments and theories in the fields of Business and Management, Economics and Finance from the leading experts at IE Business School.

Titles include:

Francisco J. López Lubián
THE EXECUTIVE GUIDE TO CORPORATE RESTRUCTURING

Faisal M. Al-Atabani and Cristina Trullols (*editors*)
SOCIAL IMPACT FINANCE

Abderrazak Belabes, Ahmed Belouafi and Cristina Trullols (*editors*)
ISLAMIC FINANCE IN WESTERN HIGHER EDUCATION

Jonathan Langton, Cristina Trullols and Abdullah Q. Turkistani (*editors*)
ISLAMIC ECONOMICS AND FINANCE

Celia de Anca
BEYOND TRIBALISM

Erik Schlie, Jörg Rheinboldt and Niko Waesche
SIMPLY SEVEN

Peter Kawalek, Boumediene Ramdani, Gastón González and Oswaldo Lorenzo
THE LONG CONVERSATION

IE Business Publishing Series
Series Standing Order ISBN: 978–0–230–29248–2

You can receive future titles in this series as they are published by placing a standing order. Please contact your bookseller or, in case of difficulty, write to us at the address below with your name and address, the title of the series and the ISBN quoted above.

Customer Services Department, Macmillan Distribution Ltd, Houndmills, Basingstoke, Hampshire RG21 6XS, England

The Executive Guide to Corporate Restructuring

The Executive Guide to Corporate Restructuring

Francisco J. López Lubián
IE Business School, Madrid, Spain

palgrave
macmillan

First published 2014 by
PALGRAVE MACMILLAN

Palgrave Macmillan in the UK is an imprint of Macmillan Publishers Limited, registered in England, company number 785998, of Houndmills, Basingstoke, Hampshire RG21 6XS.

Palgrave Macmillan in the US is a division of St Martin's Press LLC, 175 Fifth Avenue, New York, NY 10010.

Palgrave Macmillan is the global academic imprint of the above companies and has companies and representatives throughout the world.

Palgrave® and Macmillan® are registered trademarks in the United States, the United Kingdom, Europe and other countries

ISBN: 978–1–137–38935–0

This book is printed on paper suitable for recycling and made from fully managed and sustained forest sources. Logging, pulping and manufacturing processes are expected to conform to the environmental regulations of the country of origin.

A catalogue record for this book is available from the British Library.

A catalog record for this book is available from the Library of Congress.

Contents

List of Figures

List of Tables

Preface and Acknowledgements

Problem creation is a relatively easy task. Offering theoretical solutions to these problems is more difficult. But what is really difficult is to implement useful solutions to solve real problems. Any useful solution must be adequate and reasonable. An adequate solution helps to solve a real problem, according to some criteria. For example, if a company is running short of cash and the management team decides to use fate as a unique and relevant criterion, then an adequate solution to solve the problem would be to play the lottery or to bet everything at poker, expecting to win.

But an adequate solution is not necessarily reasonable. In order to be reasonable, an adequate solution must be based on reasonable criteria.

This book is about Corporate Restructuring and it tries to deal with realistic problems and to offer useful solutions. This book is the synthesis of, on the one hand, the experience of a practitioner of finance who has spent part of his professional life trying to implement useful solutions to real problems and, on the other, the academic background of a professor used to teaching finance to managers.

Since this a practical book and it uses real-life examples, a lot of people have helped me with this text. First of all, I want to thank my colleagues who reviewed part of the manuscript, suggesting new ideas and offering ideas for improvements. A special mention goes to Professor Eloy García, who patiently read all the manuscript and offered excellent suggestions. I also have to thank other friends who gave support on the data collection, such as Jaime Martínez Mosquera and Walter de Luna Butz.

Given their interest and dedication, I doubt that there are many mistakes left. Any that remain are mine.

Introduction

The world economic crisis of recent years has changed the way of life and mentality of many people, in many countries. Most people's mentality changed from an expected future of unlimited growth and enrichment, to a present dealing with loss of wealth and impoverishment, where the new norm is cost control. A change which may be characterized as a past (virtually) free lunch, to a present (almost) lack of lunch.

This change in outlook affects the priorities and dedication of many managers. Let's consider the case of CFOs attending the CFO Network conference organized by *The Wall Street Journal*, in mid-June 2013. According to the opinion of these managers, US companies should pursue objectives such as energy cost reduction, management of restructuring processes, and correct evaluation of global risks, including improvements in cybersecurity. These are very concrete objectives, in contrast with the ones pointed out in previous meetings. For example, at the beginning of the present century, CFOs were interested in more global objectives, like growth and vertical integration.

At a macro level, let's consider the case of Iceland. For reasons well-known, Iceland's banking system collapsed amid the global credit crunch. The country's currency, the krona, lost almost its entire value. Banking transactions to and from the island nation in the middle of the North Atlantic seized up, leaving its population of 320,000 virtually stranded.

As everybody knows, Iceland was just the start of a process of enormous loss of value in several countries, where trillions of US dollars were dilapidated.

These devastating effects clearly demonstrate that everybody needs a better basic understanding of how financial markets work and how sustainable economic value can be created.

Since 2007, after several *anni horribiles*, most companies are focused on restructuring and refinancing debts as a way to survive and avoid bankruptcy. Unfortunately, this is not new at all. When the value of equity becomes very close to zero, there are three main ways to increase this value (if possible):

1) Recapitalize the equity with new funds, in most cases coming from the cancellation of debt in exchange for new equity.
2) Decrease the amount of debt by selling non-core assets.
3) Increase the amount of future cash flows by implementing a restructuring plan.

As an example, let's consider the financial restructuring of Jazztel in 2002.

Jazztel was founded in 1997, in Spain, under the leadership of Martin Varsavsky, a telecoms entrepreneur. The company started operations in January 1998, and its strategy was ambitious: to be one of the strongest competitors to the former monopoly in landlines, Telefónica S.A., which was focusing operations on Spain and Portugal in order to offer a pan-Iberian network to its clients.

Implementation of Jazztel's business model implied heavy investments in a risky industry, competing in recently liberalized and evolving markets. Between 1998 and June 2002, the group had accumulated aggregate net losses of €509,212,880. The management team expected new and significant net losses for the company during the first years, as it developed its network and tried to increase the size and scope of its operations in accordance with its business plan. In the light of these losses as well as the company's financial projections, the company would not have been in a position to meet its financial obligations under the Senior Notes on an ongoing basis and, more immediately, the company would not have been in a position to pay the interest payment due on 1 October 2002 to holders of April notes. In the absence of a financial restructuring, the company would have had to cease operations in the foreseeable future, despite its achievements thus far in developing the network.

Summarizing the basic facts, on 13 June 2002, Jazztel announced that it had reached an agreement in principle with an ad hoc committee of bond holders regarding the proposed restructuring of the company's balance sheet. The proposals involved the cancellation of the Senior Notes and the release of all claims relating to the Senior Notes by their holders, in exchange for: (i) 457,334,951 new shares, representing approximately 88% of the issued share capital on the effective date, (ii) up to 18,627,092 additional shares, (iii) convertible bonds with an aggregate face value of €75 million and (iv) escrow cash, to be paid to holders of December notes only.

As a result of the financial restructuring the company managed to reduce the annual interest payments by €93 million. After the completion of the agreement, Jazztel rebalanced its financial situation allowing the company to continue to be an active player in the Spanish and Portuguese fixed-line telephone markets.

As always in these kinds of agreements, the remaining question was whether the agreement was enough to ensure the future of Jazztel. In this case, we know what happened: the recap was a stepping stone after which the company was sold. The new owners were in charge of implementing the necessary restructuring plan.

Jazztel's case points out a well-known fact: the high levels of seemingly risk-free debt assumed by families was one of the key factors leading to the financial and economic crisis that emerged in Europe and the US in 2007, along with highly leveraged banks with clients that missed payments or defaulted altogether, particularly in the real estate sector. Meanwhile, market conditions of fast-dwindling direct profits led market agents to squeeze total returns by ramping up debt levels without stopping to consider the levels of risk involved.

The terrible effects of this failure to distinguish between apparent profit and real profit are now being felt not only on a macroeconomic level (negative GDP), but also by companies (struggling for survival) and individuals (in the form of rising unemployment and falling incomes). Such inappropriate and excessive corporate debt – also the result of the incredibly strong economic growth seen previously, coupled with plentiful liquidity and negative interest rates in real terms – has now been replaced by stringent credit limits where voluntary or mandatory financial de-leveraging is the order of the day.

In recent years the continuity of many firms has been achieved by means of negotiating processes whereby liabilities can be restructured, a task which has taken up a great deal of senior management time. Companies in a wide variety of sectors have managed to survive – or not – thanks to their capacity to restructure and refinance debt.

Consider the Spanish real estate sector. The majority of companies in this industry have undergone long and difficult processes to restructure heavy debts, the result of excessive investment (leveraged), particularly in land, carried out as if demand for and prices of the finished product (housing) were set to remain at historic highs forever. The sharp drop in demand for, and prices of, all real estate assets caused immediate and dramatic financial problems for most companies in the sector, forcing them to embark on various restructuring processes with an enormous cost in terms of destruction of value for both shareholders and creditors.

The situation begs the following questions:

Does the corporate effort of restructuring serve merely to enable a firm's survival?
Can lessons be learned from these debt restructuring processes?
Is refinancing and restructuring debt the same thing?
When and how does debt restructuring happen?
How does it work?
What role does senior management play in debt restructuring?
Is it a job for specialists?
What should the main objectives be?

This book is aimed at addressing these questions and providing answers.

1
Restructuring: A General Overview

1.1 Chapter overview

A company needs a restructuring process when it is facing a situation of economic distress. A company is in a situation of economic distress when it does not generate enough cash flow to cover the payments required by its debt with financial entities.

Of course, this lack of cash to cover payments for the service of debt must be a permanent situation, since any temporary imbalance might be covered with money coming from the shareholders.

Restructuring a company means introducing changes to a company to make it viable and profitable, given that it is currently unfeasible and unprofitable. Although any corporate restructuring implies financial restructuring, it doesn't necessarily need to be only about its refinancing. The objective of any restructuring is to implement changes in the company so that it will generate enough FCF to cover the service of debt and remunerate its shareholders satisfactorily.

A restructuring process is a process of negotiation. As in all negotiating processes it is important to understand the interests of all the parties involved, recognizing their strong points and weak points, their negotiating clout, and so on.

1.2 What is restructuring?

A company is in need of a restructuring process when it faces a situation of economic and/or financial distress. A company is in distress when generated cash flow is insufficient to cover its debt payments due. In other words, a company is in a situation of economic distress when its operating cash flow is not enough to cover its debt service. Restructuring is therefore a negotiated process whereby a company optimizes operations and adapts financial and trade payments aspects to its cash flow generating capacity.

Since restructuring is related to cash flow generation, let's define in a more precise way what we mean by cash flow.

Technically, a company is in distress when its Free Cash Flow (FCF) is lower than the payments needed to service its maturing debt: financial expenses after taxes and amortization of the debt's principal. By FCF we mean the money generated by the company's operating activities of the company (that is, coming from the management of all the operational aspects included in the Profit and Loss and Operational Assets). Table 1.1 summarizes the definition of FCF and its principal components.

Figure 1.1 depicts a situation of distress: the FCF is lower than cash needed to cover financial obligations. The company is therefore in a situation where operating cash is insufficient to attend all the payments related to the service of the debt. This FCF has three components, reflecting the sources of the operational activities of any company: operational activities coming from (i) the day-to-day management of operations as reflected in the P and L; (ii) from the management of day-to-day operations reflected in the operational working capital; and (iii) from the medium and long-term operational decisions reflected in the Capex.

Certainly, this lack of FCF to cover debt service must be assumed to be a permanent situation, since any temporary imbalance might be covered with funds from the shareholders. Conversely, if the situation is assumed to be permanent, the company is not feasible (or viable) from an economic point of view, unless shareholders cover this gap with an unlimited supply of new funds. This permanent imbalance can be past or expected.

Having established the conditions for economic feasibility, we can now turn to economic profitability.

From an economic perspective, if a company generates enough FCF to cover the service of the debt, could we say, from an economic point of view,

Table 1.1 How to calculate the Free Cash Flow

Earnings before Interest and Taxes (EBIT)
– Taxes on EBIT
= Earnings Before Interest and after Taxes (EBIaT)
+ Depreciation
= Free Cash Flow (FCF) from operational P and L (excluding interest expenses)
+/– FCF from variation in Operational Working Capital (Net Current Assets)
+/– FCF from variation in Fixed Assets (Capex)
= Total FCF

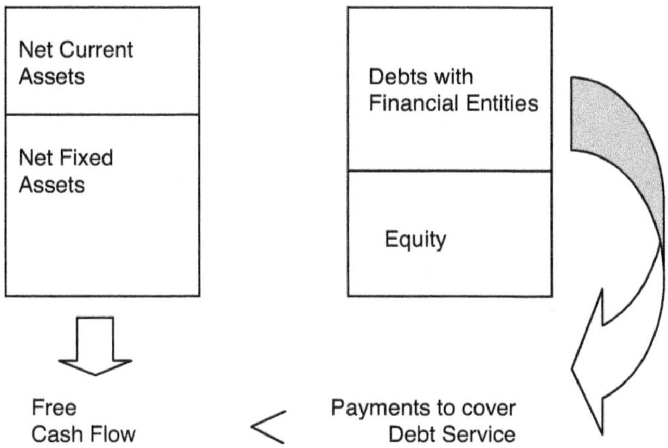

Where:

Net Current Assets = Current Assets – Current Liabilities (excluding short term debt)

Net Fixed Assets = Gross Fixed Assets – Accumulated Depreciation

Equity = Capital + Accumulated Reserves

Figure 1.1 A situation of distress

that the company is sustainable? Not really, unless its shareholders agree to lose all their invested funds. Consequently, a company can ensure its continuity only if it generates enough FCF to be feasible and to compensate its shareholders with money that will create in them a certain expected economic profitability. In any company, economic sustainability means that the company will generate enough FCF to be feasible and profitable.

Restructuring a company means introducing changes to a company to make it viable and profitable, given that the company is currently unfeasible and unprofitable. Although any corporate restructuring implies financial restructuring, it doesn't necessarily need to be only about its refinancing. The objective of any restructuring is to implement changes in the company so that it will generate enough FCF to cover the service of debt and remunerate its shareholders satisfactorily.

Note that by profitability we refer to economic profitability, not accounting profitability. Accounting profitability is normally measured with a ratio like ROE (Return on Equity), defined as a ratio of Earnings to Book Equity. Conversely, economic profitability is related to real money (cash flow) that the shareholders receive. Specifically, economic profitability is measured by the Internal Rate of Return (IRR) of the FCF to shareholders, meaning the FCF left after covering all the payments related to the service of the debt. See Table 1.2.

Furthermore, restructuring comprises the implementation of improvements in the scope of the firm, its asset management and Capital Structure; it is not only a matter of changing the terms and conditions of the debts.

The following numerical example will help to clarify these points. Let's consider the case of Publications, Inc., a multimedia company that provides e-learning services.

Table 1.3 summarizes the evolution of some key figures of the company in the last 5 years.

It's clear that FCF every year is the amount of money available to finance (or to be financed, if negative) total service of debt. As a result, total debt goes to 4,275 at the end of 2013, from 980 at the beginning of 2008. This depicts a company with serious problems of economic feasibility and profitability. Of economic feasibility because its negative FCF may not always be (will be) financed with an increase in debt. Of economic profitability because the company does not reward its shareholders at all.

Table 1.4 shows this reality, in which FCF to shareholders every year is 0.

Table 1.2 From FCF of the firm to FCF to the shareholders

Total FCF
+/– Amortization of the Principal
– Interest Expenses × (1–t)
= FCF to Shareholders

Table 1.3 Key figures for Publications, Inc. (figures in thousands of euros)

Years	**2008**	**2009**	**2010**	**2011**	**2012**	**2013**
Revenues	12,277	12,639	11,958	11,588	11,446	10,856
EBIT	512	525	394	365	305	221
Taxes on EBIT	–128	–131	–99	–91	–76	–55
EBIaT	384	394	296	274	229	166
Depreciation	333	324	325	346	363	327
FCL from P and L	717	718	621	620	592	493
FCL from Operating WC	222	–246	–624	143	–491	474
FCL from Capex	–1,368	–1,221	–1,435	–684	–338	–850
Total FCF	–429	–749	–1,439	79	–237	117
Debt Evolution						
Initial Debt	980	1,446	2,249	3,772	3,835	4,216
Final Debt	1,446	2,249	3,772	3,835	4,216	4,257

Table 1.4 Expected Equity Cash Flow evolution (Figures in thousands of euros)

Years	**Initial**	**2008**	**2009**	**2010**	**2011**	**2012**	**2013**
Net Current Assets	800	578	824	1,448	1,305	1,796	1,322
Net Fixed Assets	1,180	2,215	3,112	4,222	4,560	4,535	5,058
Total Net Assets	1,980	2,793	3,936	5,670	5,865	6,331	6,380
Total Debt	980	1,446	2,249	3,772	3,835	4,216	4,257
EQUITY	1,000	1,347	1,687	1,898	2,030	2,115	2,123
Total D+E	1,980	2,793	3,936	5,670	5,865	6,331	6,380
EBIT		512	525	394	365	305	221
F. Expenses		–49	–72	–112	–189	–192	–211
EBT		463	455	282	176	113	10
Taxes		–116	–113	–70	–44	–28	–3
Net earnings		347	340	211	132	85	8
To Reserves		347	340	211	132	85	8
FCF		–429	–749	–1439	79	–237	117
F Exp. (1–t)		–37	–54	–84	–141	–144	–158
Evolut. Princip. of Debt		466	803	1523	63	381	41
FCF to Shareholders		0	0	0	0	0	0

Table 1.5 Expected evolution of ROE

Years	**2008**	**2009**	**2010**	**2011**	**2012**	**2013**	**Average ROE**
ROE	25.80%	20.10%	11.10%	6.50%	4.00%	0.40%	11.30%

Note that accounting profitability[1] of Publications, Inc. during this period is always positive, with an average ROE of 11.3% (see Table 1.5). Again, economic profitability differs from accounting profitability. The former shows how a company can produce attractive ratios in accounting terms while the economic reality of the firm is approaching distress. In the case of Publications, Inc. it is due to declining funds from operations that have been compensated with a constant increase in financial debt. This is a sign typical of weak profitability and financial vulnerability which, in the end, may require a restructuring. In short, economic health (viability and profitability) of a company must be analysed in economic and not accounting terms.

1.3 When is restructuring about to happen?

Publications, Inc. needs a restructuring because the company is not economically and financially sustainable. And this is so because it is neither economically viable nor profitable, in spite of the average accounting profitability for its shareholders being 11.3%.

How can this happen? At what point does a restructuring of a company become needed?

We already know the answer. It's when a company does not generate enough FCF to cover the payments required to meet the requirements of the debt and/or the shareholders. This structural lack of cash may find its roots in the operational side of the company, and/or in the capital structure.

The operational causes that might produce a permanent lack of FCF are generally:

1) Errors in defining the scope of the firm.
2) Management and strategic errors. Inadequacy of products, markets or core capacities. Inadequate definition of competitive advantage.
3) Excess of operational leverage. Excessive operating vulnerability.
4) Poor management of operational working capital.
5) Overinvestment. Investment errors.
6) Agency costs: conflict of interest among managers, shareholders, creditors.

The financial causes that might produce a permanent lack of cash are:

1) Excess financial leverage.
2) Lack of analysis of debt capacity and optimal capital structure.
3) Financing errors.

Consequently, the needed restructuring process of Publications, Inc. should be separated in two: operating restructuring and financing restructuring. This will allow it to deal with the operational and financial causes of the problem.

In this chapter we will discuss about restructuring from a general point of view, making no specific distinction between operating and financing restructuring. In the coming chapters we'll discuss these topics more in depth.

1.4 When is a restructuring needed?

Keeping in mind the above comments, we may now summarize that a restructuring of a company's total debt results from two major reasons:

a) serious liquidity issues resulting from a significant fall in income and/or from a substantial rise in costs that threaten the company's capacity to meet its operational and financial commitments in the short term; and

b) a severe drop in the market value of the company's strategic assets, which in turn impacts the collateral value of the assets vis-a-vis specific financing packages.

1.5 What does a restructuring entail?

The key aim of a debt restructuring process is to reach a private agreement on the future terms and conditions of the firm's debts in order to render the company viable in the face of an ongoing or imminent lack of funds. Broadly speaking, it is about agreeing on how the company's cash flow can be distributed among the different providers of funds and other creditors so as to avoid bankruptcy or a liquidation process that would be overly burdensome for the different economic and social agents involved. Most likely a restructuring will include measures to optimize the scope of the firm and its cash flow generating aspects.

It is possible to draw up a series of key characteristics based on this premise:

1) A restructuring process consists of reaching a private agreement in order to prevent legal proceedings. It is also possible to base the agreement on corresponding bankruptcy law, although it would have to be under judicial protection and subject to regulations that are often more rigid (e.g. a creditors' agreement).
2) A restructuring is a special refinancing agreement for when a payment plan has not been met (distress), rather than the simple refinancing process used when there is no financial tension.
3) The objective is to render the company viable and to ensure its continuity.
4) It only makes sense if the value of the debt is greater after the restructuring than the value of the company in liquidation.
5) It is assumed that certain operational restructuring measures have already been implemented, but proved insufficient to generate the required cash flow to avoid financial distress.

Figure 1.2 shows the different scenarios that may occur in a company that needs to restructure its debt.

Unlike in an ordinary refinancing process, in which a company undertakes a bilateral negotiation with banks in a context of several possible alternatives, debt restructuring involves a large number of social and economic

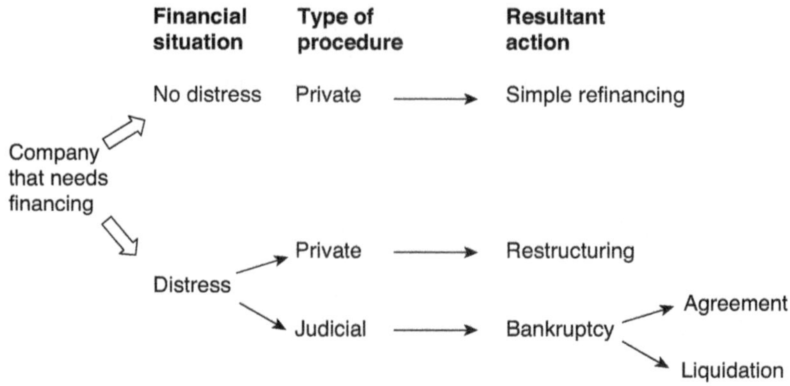

Figure 1.2 Debt restructuring scenarios

agents interacting in a situation in which there are few alternatives to be considered under great time pressure. The debt restructuring affects every aspect of the company and has a deep impact on its future viability. As stated above, the survival of the firm depends on it.

Debt restructuring affects both finance and trade creditors, along with shareholders, employees and clients, as well as the tax authorities and other public sector institutions. The restructuring and viability plan has to seek a balance between the cost of securing viability for the firm and the sacrifices that all the different parties involved would have to make if the firm were to fail. This would result in a costly liquidation process with heavy losses for all those affected.

It is not difficult to imagine the enormous technical and operational difficulties that a process of this kind would involve, not only because of the large number of affected parties, but also due to obvious conflicts of interest.

Figure 1.3 can help us understand the different relations and interests involved in a debt restructuring process.

What tools do the different agents have at their disposal to align their credit rights with the (reduced) cash flows that can be expected from a firm under these stressful circumstances? How is the restructuring process decided? Table 1.6 shows the contributions that economic agents often have to make to ensure the continuity of the company.

As Table 1.6 shows, parties involved are required to reduce the current value of their rights (delays and greater risk) to ensure the continuity of the company (liquidity) in order to avoid the worst case scenario: bankruptcy and liquidation with far greater losses.

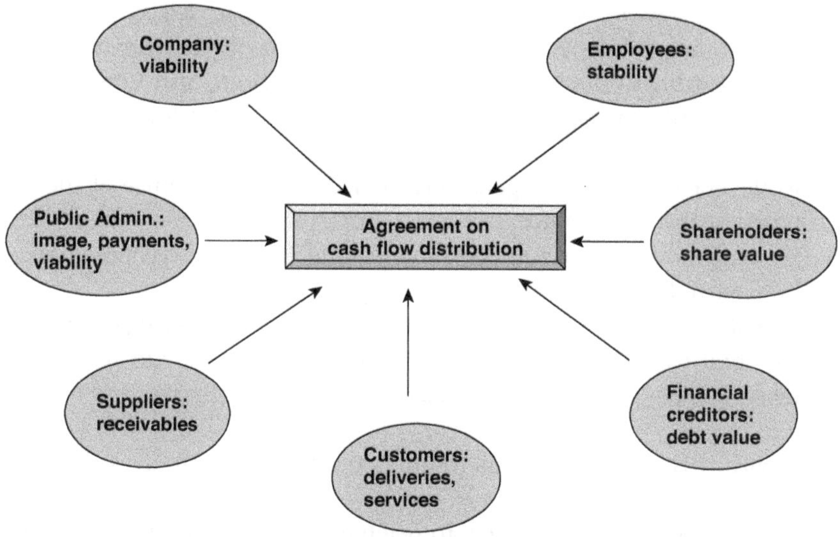

Figure 1.3 Elements that comprise a restructuring process

Table 1.6 Main contributions from economic agents to ensure a company's continuity

Agent	Actions	Objectives
Public administration	Extend payment deadlines	
Trade creditors	Extend payment deadlines, cancel debt	
Clients	Extend delivery deadlines	
Employees	Reduce workforce, reduce/freeze wages	Improved cash flows, particularly in the short and medium term
Financial creditors	Extend payment deadlines, reduce interest rates, supply new funds, capitalization	
Shareholders	Supply new funds, waive dividends	
Company	Reduce investments, reduce operational costs, modify strategic planning	

Hence, when a company finds itself in a distress situation, it has two alternatives:

1) Reaching an agreement to restructure the debt by means of a private procedure.
2) Filing for bankruptcy (insolvency filing), which will result in either an insolvency agreement or liquidation.

Let's take the case of Famosa, a Spanish company founded in 1957 and a leader in the Spanish toy market, with a market share of approximately 8.2%. At the beginning of 2009 the company faced a serious cash flow problem and it was highly leveraged. This situation was largely due to:

1) Two leveraged purchase operations carried out in the course of the first decade of the millennium.
2) The acquisition of an outdoor vehicles and toys firm (Feber) financed 100% with debt.
3) The volatile funding needs of seasonally-dependent working capital.
4) Deteriorating credit markets and tight liquidity in the credit system.
5) Lower levels of consumerism and a downturn in the market and in sales.

Faced with this scenario, Famosa found two strategic alternatives:

i. Call a creditors meeting to try to reach a judicial solution, which could comprise any of three possible alternatives: insolvency agreement, distress sale, or liquidation of the company.
ii. Initiate the debt restructuring process, designed to provide the company with stability to make it viable, in order to later sell it.

Having examined these strategic alternatives, it was decided that the value of Famosa in a state of liquidation was very low. Hence, even though recognizing that the process would be highly complex, it was decided that the best option was to embark on a debt restructuring in order to subsequently sell the company.

1.6 Key phases of a restructuring process

Any corporate debt restructuring includes both internal and external actions, which can be summarized as follows:

1.6.1 Internal actions

1) Identification of a liquidity problem: why, how much and when.
2) Preparation of an internal funding plan:
   a) Short-term treasury plan
   b) Medium and long-term profit plan.
3) Negotiation strategy with a bank pool and other agents: what the company offers, to whom, and in what conditions.
4) Preliminary proposal to the bank pool.

1.6.2 External actions

The external actions of a debt restructuring process are designed to secure agreements among the parties, by identifying negotiators and possible settlements, appointing experts in relevant legal and technical fields, and by agreeing on follow-up mechanisms to monitor the fulfilment of agreements.[2]

Such activities include:

1) Bilateral negotiations with members of the pool.
2) Coordination and negotiation with the agent bank and the bank pool steering committee.
3) Identification of general and specific guarantees.
4) Legal review of contracts and clauses.
5) Data room for legal documents and accounting information.
6) Final negotiations and signing.
7) Follow-up and monitoring.

It is important to establish within a global negotiation plan the order in which the company approaches its creditors, starting with those that wield the greatest potential power in the negotiating process. Consider, for example, the trade creditors: they can totally block operations and easily take the firm into bankruptcy by pushing for small amounts, thus causing enormous losses for financial creditors. Hence the most that is generally demanded of trade creditors in the corporate restructuring process is that they extend payment deadlines, and negotiations tend to focus initially on financial creditors. The financial creditor will usually permit, or even fund, the payment of suppliers in order to guarantee the company's operational continuity while it renegotiates to maximize the probabilities of recouping the money it has lent. The shareholders, meanwhile, will try to limit payment to financial creditors, or even seek to continue diverting cash flow to new investments in order to protect share value.

Occasionally, as described below, this conflict of interest can be resolved by placing financial creditors in the dual position of shareholder and lender, in which case the debate will then revolve around the price of exchanging debt for shares.

Nevertheless, not all financial creditors are in the same position vis-á-vis the company. The specific position of each depends basically on four things:

1) the amount of money owed to them;
2) guarantees (if the debt is secured or not);

3) precedence (senior or subordinate); and
4) optionality (convertibility).

Obviously, the senior creditor owed a guaranteed debt is far less likely to give up any rights contained in its finance agreements compared to a subordinate creditor with no guarantee. Moreover, creditors owed debts of a relatively low amount that are due in the near future may be in a stronger position, even if the debts are not guaranteed, given that non-fulfilment of such a payment could cause considerable losses for other creditors that are owed larger amounts. It is not unusual to see banks which stand to lose large amounts 'buy' smaller debts owed to other creditors to gain control over the restructuring process. From the company's perspective, it is important to carry out a detailed analysis of the impact that defaulting on any one of its debts could have on remaining creditors and shareholders, if it is to draw up a negotiating plan that has a chance of succeeding.

Which agreements cover the results of the series of negotiations that form part of debt restructuring? Basically there are four:

1) New temporary scheduling of payment deadlines, types of debt (precedence and guarantees) and renegotiation of associated costs. This measure is typical when there is a more or less temporary drop in the revenues of the company, which is still considered viable.
2) Conversion of debt into capital (capitalization) in return for adhering to conditions (policy-related or restriction of dividends). This measure is applied when there is excessive debt that cannot be paid off in the long term but the company is worth more if it continues to operate than if it goes into liquidation.
3) A spin off (change of recourse). For example: separation from the 'bad company'. This alternative is used in situations similar to those described in point 2, coupled with the intention to sell or attract new investors to the 'good company'.
4) A business plan that lists, among other things, the operational costs of investments. It could include new lines of liquidity for short-term and medium-term purposes (new money) which will generally be given super seniority.

Coming back to the case of Famosa, the debt restructuring process referred to earlier took six months to negotiate and included the following points:

i. Funding needs of some €30 million, partially covered by an injection of new money totalling some €17 million. Consideration of *super senior debt*, both in terms of guarantees and cost.
ii. Renegotiation of an old debt (some €200 million) with an average write off of 65%.
iii. Design of a new finance structure, with long-term incentives for debtors (recovery of liquidation value).
iv. Complex crossed option systems that enabled a subsequent forced sale (with deduction) subject to forming majorities.

1.7 Key points in negotiation

A debt restructuring process is a negotiation process. As in all negotiations it is a good idea to be able to understand the interests of the different parties involved, as well as their weak and strong points, bargaining power, potential conflicts, etc.

In effect, there are three main parties involved in debt restructuring: the banks, the company's senior management and the shareholders. They all have different interests, given that banks are mainly worried about the viability of the company and how it is going to repay its debt, while management is chiefly interested in the continuity of the company and securing their positions, and shareholders just want to know about growth and plans for the future. Table 1.7 provides a summary of this scenario.

One of the big aims in the discussion will be to map out a realistic plan for the future, in which the expected FCF that will ensure short-term viability is enough to finance the medium- and long-term needs of the company, without a limit for the investment needed to ensure the continuity of the business.

Table 1.7 Conflicts of interest among the parties

Participant	Interests	Conflict with
Banks	Feasibility	Long-term vision
	Repayment of debt	Continuity, shareholders
	Reduction of credit risk	Trade creditors
Shareholders	Growth	Short-term vision
	Equity store	Credit risk, financial creditors
	Future of the company	Tax authorities
Management team	Continuity	Short-term viability
	Maintenance of position	Profitability (shareholders)
		Financial creditors

In short, it is about reaching agreements on how the company can generate liquidity in both quantitative and qualitative terms. More specifically:

What is the composition of the free cash flow?
How much is there?
Is it sustainable over time?
Where is this cash flow allocated?
What is the company giving up in order to achieve this liquidity?

Let's not forget either that a realistic plan for the future should take into account both the direct and indirect bargaining power of all the parties involved.

Consider, for example the role of its trade creditors mentioned above. The commercial creditors of a company in a distress situation tend to be far more dispersed, and subject to far less individual risk than the banks. Hence, the trade creditors can have far more chances of taking the company to court and of rendering a restructuring process non-viable (or at least making it a great deal more difficult). In these cases, those trade creditors have far more negotiating clout than the banks. Accordingly, the viability plan agreed with the banks must take into consideration this reality, which means that the free cash flow should include eventual payment to these creditors.

1.8 The advantages of a restructuring process

The possibilities of carrying out a successful debt restructuring process depend to a great extent on which of the parties involved accept the agreements as a way to move from a situation where loss is the order of the day to a situation where all parties stand to gain, at least relatively speaking.

As stated earlier, the first step when negotiating a restructuring process is to convince all parties that the value of a restructured company is greater than the value it would produce if liquidated. In order to achieve this it is vital to secure an agreement among the different parties with regard to how much money is needed for future cash flows, and how it will be distributed.

In addition to these basic points, when negotiating a debt restructuring process it is a good idea to discuss and agree on the other advantages associated with the process, which can help the parties accept proposed solutions as an eventual business opportunity.

Table 1.8 summarizes some of the advantages that can be highlighted in a debt restructuring process.

Table 1.8 Advantages associated with a debt restructuring process

For the management team	For the banks	For the shareholders
The financial structure is designed in accordance with the capacity of the company to generate cash flow.	Greater probability of recovering the theoretical value derived from liquidation.	The eventual exit will be in an orderly fashion, minimizing reputational risk.
Liquidation is avoided. Stability and eventual continuity.	Possibility of recovering greater value than in the case of liquidation.	Avoids investment in assets in which they are no longer interested.
A new phase starts in which generating cash flow and creating value is given priority (motivation).	Greater influence on future decision making through, for example, the creation of majorities.	The upside potential is maintained.

1.9 Summary

Over the last few years, the continuity of a large number of companies has depended at some time on a debt restructuring process to which the senior management of the firms in question have dedicated a considerable effort and time. In short, companies in highly diverse sectors have survived – or gone under – as a result of their capacity (or incapacity) to restructure and refinance their debts.

A company needs a restructuring process when it is facing a situation of economic distress. A company is in a situation of economic distress when it does not generate enough cash flow to cover the payments required by its debt with financial entities.

Of course, this lack of cash to cover payments to service debt must be a permanent situation, since any temporary imbalance might be covered with money coming from the shareholders.

Restructuring a company means introducing changes to a company to make it viable and profitable, given that the company is currently unfeasible and unprofitable. Although any corporate restructuring implies financial restructuring, it doesn't necessarily need to be only about its refinancing. The objective of any restructuring is to implement changes in the company so that it will generate enough FCF to cover the service of debt and remunerate its shareholders satisfactorily.

A restructuring process is a process of negotiation. As in all negotiating processes it is important to understand the interests of all the parties involved, recognizing their strong points and weak points, their negotiating clout, and so on.

And, of course, it is important to know the answers to key questions, like:

Why did it happen?
What are the main debt restructuring actions that need to be taken?
What advantages will the debt restructuring process bring to the different parties involved?
What can the company offer to reach agreements in which everybody gains?

The key to success in any restructuring process is to reach an agreement whereby the value of the restructured company is greater than it would be if it were wound down, and then to agree on how this greater value should be distributed. One of the most important points for discussion is that of agreeing on a realistic plan for the future, and ensuring that securing sufficient free cash flow for short-term viability does not jeopardize the firm's medium- and long-term future by limiting investment plans that are essential for the continuity of the business.

2
Steps in Restructuring

2.1 Chapter overview

Corporate financial restructuring involves activities both inside and outside the company. These actions taken within the company basically comprise:

- Defining the liquidity problem: why, how much and when.
- Preparing an internal financial plan, including a short-term treasury plan and a plan for medium- and long-term profitability.
- Strategy for negotiations with the group of banks: what do we offer, to whom and under what conditions?
- Preliminary proposal to put to the group of financial institutions.

The external actions involved in a financial restructuring process are aimed at achieving agreements between the parties, by identifying negotiators and possible arbiters, appointing experts for technical and legal matters, and establishing monitoring mechanisms so as to ensure compliance with the agreements.

As these external actions are carried out involving the banks, it is worth distinguishing between external actions with the banks' commercial area and external actions with their technical area.

2.2 Introduction

In the previous chapter we discussed how a crisis can undermine trust in plans for the future and can also precipitate a liquidity squeeze that puts the economic viability of many companies in serious jeopardy. In this context, as we have seen, the key to survival lies in the ability to restructure and refinance debt.

We will now describe more in detail the different steps that are necessary to follow to implement a corporate restructuring. These involve activities both inside and outside the company. We will first look at the actions taken within the company in some detail.

2.3 Corporate restructuring: internal actions

These comprise basically of:

1. Defining the liquidity problem: why, how bad is the shortfall and when?
2. Preparing an internal financial plan, specifying a short-term treasury plan as well as a plan for medium- and long-term profitability.
3. Determining a strategy for negotiating with the group of banks: what to offer, to whom and under what conditions?
4. Drawing up a preliminary proposal to present to the group of financial institutions.

2.3.1 Defining the liquidity problem

Why do liquidity problems arise? When a problem arises the most typical reaction is to deny that the problem exists. This denial may take many forms, ranging from considering that 'it does not affect me' to blaming it that on 'someone else'.

The first step in any restructuring process is avoiding falling into this trap. In fact, although it is usually evident when a company has a liquidity problem, it is surprising how often its existence is denied or the blame is shifted on to others (it is often argued that it is 'due to a lack of support from the banks').

Therefore, the fundamental process of the restructuring must start by recognizing that there is a liquidity problem, identifying and analysing its causes, and putting forward alternative possible solutions to overcome it.

A company's liquidity can come from the following four main sources:

- Liquidity generated from operational sources relating to the profit and loss account. This is the liquidity that is generated – or consumed – through the company's applying its short-term operating policies, as reflected on the profit and loss statement (P and L). These include its pricing policy, margins, cost control, operating costs, salaries and compensation, etc. We will refer to this here as the Net Cash Flow coming from the P and L.
- Liquidity (positive or negative) generated by operating aspects of the company's management of working capital (WC). This will normally include customer collection policies, payment terms for suppliers,

inventory management, operating treasury positions, etc. We will call it the Net Cash Flow coming from operational WC.
- Liquidity generated from implementing the company's plan of investment in fixed assets, which could also take the form of divestments. We will call this the Net Cash Flow coming from investments in Fixed Assets.
- Liquidity arising from the company's capital compensation policy, and the policy of obtaining funding from equity. We will call this the Net Cash Flow coming from Capital.

Accordingly, the Total Net Cash Flow (NCF) becomes the sum of these four components, which must be equal to the change in the amount of debt outstanding.

In the last chapter we defined the company's Free Cash Flow (FCF) as the liquidity generated from all of its operational activities (originated from the management of all of its operational aspects associated with its Profit and Loss and Operational Assets). In turn, we will now define the Net Cash Flow (NCF) as the liquidity generated by all of its operational activities (including interest expenses) as well as from its Equity. Table 2.1 summarizes the differences between the two, NCF and FCF.

Table 2.1 Differences between NCF and FCF

Net Cash Flow (NCF)	**Free Cash Flow (FCF)**
Earnings before Taxes (EBT)	Earnings before Interests and Taxes (EBIT)
– Tax Expenses (on EBT)	– Tax Expenses (on EBIT)
= Net Earnings	= EBIaT
+ Depreciation Expenses	+ Depreciation Expenses
= NCF from Operations	= FCF from Operations
+/– Investments in Operating WC	+/– Investments in Operating WC
+/– Investments in Fixed Assets (Capex)	+/– Investments in Fixed Assets (Capex)
+/– Variations in Equity	
= Total Net Cash Flow	= Total Free Cash Flow
NCF is the liquidity generated in a company, independently of the variation in total Debt.	FCF is the liquidity generated from the Assets, independently of how it is financed.
NCF = Variation in total Debt	FCF = Liquidity from Assets
Focus: How debt will be paid	Focus: Liquidity from Assets
NCF: Cash generated from Operational activities and Equity (including interest expenses)	FCF: Cash generated from Operational activities (excluding interest expenses)

Let's return again to the case of the company Publications, Inc., analysed in the previous chapter. We have to bear in mind that, in the last six years, the company has been facing a very serious economic feasibility problem, since the liquidity generated from its assets was negative during four years. Table 2.2 summarizes the evolution of Publications' Net Cash Flow during 2008–2013.

When we examine liquidity from this perspective, the following conclusions emerge:

- Debt reduction through amortization is only achieved by generating positive net cash flow (NCF). Notice that in the case of Publications, Inc., the increase in debt during the period 2008–2013 is due to the negative Net Cash Flow generated.
- A company in a permanent state of negative NCF is economically unsustainable.
- The total short-term liquidity generated by a company is the sum of its Net Cash Flow generated by short-term operating activities (P and L and WC), while the long-term liquidity is the sum of its Net Cash Flow generated by Investments in FA and Capital. In the case of our company, it generated 2,619 thousand euros from short-term sources during 2008–2013, and it invested 5,896 thousand euros in Capex.

Table 2.2 Evolution of Net Cash Flow (Figures in thousands of euros)

Years	2008	2009	2010	2011	2012	2013	Total Period
Net Earnings	347	340	211	132	85	8	1,123
Depreciation	333	324	325	346	363	327	2,018
Net Cash Flow from P and L	680	664	536	478	448	335	3,141
Net Cash Flow coming from Operating WC	222	–246	–624	143	–491	474	–522
Net Cash Flow coming from Investments in FA	–1,368	–1,221	–1,435	–684	–338	–850	–5,896
Net Cash Flow coming from Capital	0	0	0	0	0	0	0
Total Net Cash Flow	–466	–803	–1,523	–63	–381	–41	–3,277
Variation in Debt	466	803	1,523	63	381	41	3,277

- Understanding if the problem is caused by a short- or long-term liquidity shortage, and whether it is of a recurrent nature or not, is crucial to understanding the root of the company's liquidity problem. Short-term problems call for different solutions than long-term ones. The former tend to be a recurring issue, whereas the latter are temporary or associated with very specific phases in the life of the business. The former would need short-term finance, and the latter should be financed from long-term borrowings.
- Although it is normally easy to identify if a company has an inherent liquidity problem, it is surprising to find how often its existence is denied or the blame is shifted on to others
- Consequently, it becomes not only a matter of generating positive NCF, but of analysing its sustainability over time as well. In this regard, the condition of Publications, Inc. would be very different if the imbalance between the liquidity generated from short- and long-term sources were a temporary or a permanent situation.
- Under the assumption of a permanently self-financing company, the liquidity generated in the short-term would be that amount to be allocated to finance long-term policies: that is, its investments and return on capital. Accordingly, its NCF would be zero.

2.3.2 Preparing a short- and a long-term financing plan

After the liquidity problem is identified, it becomes necessary to restructure and refinance the company. This requires the preparation of a short- and a long-term financing plan, including those operational measures that need to be put in place to improve operating liquidity in the short, medium and long-term, together with the associated resources that will be needed to ensure the company's viability.

Short-term viability usually requires a restructuring of the liabilities, for example converting debt into equity, refinancing debt or deferring maturities. Obviously, the conditions under which the liabilities are restructured, as well as the new resulting maturities, must be consistent with the steps taken by the company to improve those operations that generate fresh liquidity to support its future viability and economic value.

Table 2.3 shows an example of a proposed restructuring of liabilities through a refinancing with new maturities and under new conditions.

Moreover, the proposed plan must be integrated in time with the short-term plan, as shown in Table 2.4.

Table 2.3 An example of restructuring

Proposed operation	Sources	Uses
Short-term debts		
Credit policies		−12,125,478
Total cash need		−65,897,465
Total		−78,022,943
Long-term debts		
Syndicated loans tranche A (transformation of credit policies)	15,879,454	
Total cash need	62,143,489	
Total	78,022,943	

Notes:

- The objective of the proposed operation is to change the maturity of Group X's financial debt to match it with the maturities of investments made over the last five years.
- The proposed sources of funds will be provided by long-term debt, divided into two tranches, with maturities of seven years and a two-year grace period.
- The long-term debt resulting from this restructuring implies a ratio of three times the forecast EBITDA (earnings before interest, taxes, depreciation and amortization) for 2009. If both short- and long-term loans are taken into account, the ratio will be 3.5 times EBITDA.
- The proceeds from all disposals of assets under the asset-restructuring plan will be devoted to the reduction of debt finance through the pool of banks.
- The replenishment of its working capital will allow the group to set up a business platform with a sustainable capital structure.

Table 2.4 Integration of the short- and long-term financing plans

Total requirements	September 2011	October 2011	November 2011	December 2011	Total
Proposed drawdowns	−20,425,201	−6,254,125	−3,255,000	−8,546,233	−38,480,559
Tranche 1					
Tranche 2	6,543,214			8,546,233	15,089,447
Tranche 3	1,564,798	6,254,125			7,818,923
Tranche 4	12,317,189				12,317,189
			3,255,000		3,255,000
Total drawdowns	20,425,201	6,254,125	3,255,000	8,546,233	38,480,559
Cumulative total	20,425,201	26,679,326	29,934,326	38,480,559	

2.3.3 Strategy to negotiate with the banks

Before starting to negotiate with the banks (existing or news), management must define its negotiation strategy in terms of the specific requests to be made and the guarantees it may be able to offer in exchange.

This is the moment at which to set out a proposal on how the possible refinancing is going to be distributed, under what conditions, and subject to what limits and guarantees. By way of example, Table 2.5 shows the security and collateral pledged for the proposed refinancing.

Furthermore, the negotiating strategy and tactics should include identification of the negotiable points, possible counter-proposals from the banks, matters kept in reserve (if possible) to be raised during the process, etc.

2.3.4 Preliminary proposal

Based on the foregoing, an initial proposal may now be drawn up for submission to the bank or banks involved in the operation, breaking down their specific financial interests, risks, guarantees, etc. The criteria according to which the breakdown of the operation is made need to be clearly defined. In Table 2.6 we can see an example of how to set out this type of proposal.

Table 2.5 Security associated with a refinancing proposal

Type	Valuations
Valuations performed	15,000,002.38
Valuations pending	22,678,500.01
Shares as collateral	78,852,636.49
Concessions	14,289,112.00
Other guarantees	5,480,000.00
Total guarantees	136,300,250.90

Table 2.6 Example of preliminary proposal to the group of financial institutions

Institution	Percentage of risk	Accumulated risk	Finance (euros)	Adjusted funding	Accumulated risk	Liquidity (euros)
Bank 1	21.00%	21.00%	11,550,000.00	24.52%	24.52%	13,483,486.49
Bank 2	15.00%	36.00%	8,250,000.00	14.73%	39.24%	8,100,271.58
Bank 3	10.93%	46.93%	6,012,026.49	11.48%	50.73%	6,316,267.97
Bank 4	8.00%	54.93%	4,400,000.00	9.65%	60.38%	5,307,762.42
Bank 5	7.88%	62.81%	4,335,134.87	8.28%	68.66%	4,554,516.45
Bank 6	7.00%	69.81%	3,850,000.00	6.76%	75.42%	3,717,121.78
Bank 7	6.50%	76.31%	3,575,000.00	6.62%	82.04%	3,640,390.45
Bank 8	5.39%	81.70%	2,965,235.17	5.66%	87.70%	3,115,292.32
Bank 9	6.00%	87.70%	3,300,000.00	4.44%	92.14%	2,443,381.57
Bank 10	3.74%	91.44%	2,056,918.88	3.93%	96.07%	2,161,010.25
Bank 11	2.62%	94.07%	1,442,204.69	2.75%	98.83%	1,515,188.15
Bank 12	0.18%	94.25%	98,354.27			
Bank 13	1.64%	95.89%	904,421.07			
Bank 14	0.00%	95.89%	0.00			
Bank 15	1.43%	97.32%	786,103.81			
Bank 16	1.46%	98.78%	802,415.04			
Bank 17	1.12%	99.89%	614,227.29	1.17%	100.00%	645,310.55
Bank 18	0.03%	100.00%	15,597.92			
	100.00%		55,000,000.00			55,000,000.00

2.4 Corporate restructuring: external actions

The external actions required in a corporate restructuring process are aimed at achieving agreements among the parties, by appointing negotiators and possible arbiters, experts for technical and legal matters, and agreeing and setting up monitoring mechanisms to ensure compliance with the agreements.

As all these external actions are carried, it is worth differentiating between those external actions falling within the banks' commercial area and those external actions falling within its technical area.

2.4.1 Initial actions with the banks' commercial area

Restructuring formally commences when the restructuring proposal is presented to the institutions forming the bank pool.

At the initial meeting, the company's financial condition is clearly outlined together with the proposed solutions, and the required new financing. This is a particularly crucial and stressful moment for all of the institutions concerned with the restructuring. As such, the problem needs to be analysed exhaustively in order to reach a solution that ensures the company's viability.

Subsequent preliminary meetings are to be held at the bank's sales offices, since it is the branches who are the ones required to send the initial information back to regional management and the relevant risk department. At this point it will be necessary to decide which of the institutions is going to lead the restructuring process. Normally, the institution that holds the largest share of risk is the one selected as lead agent bank. The restructuring department at that bank will be responsible for coordinating all meetings and information.

After the provisional proposal has incorporated the contributions from all the participant institutions, a definitive proposal may be drawn up and circulated among the pertinent risk departments.

Once the last draft of the proposal has been finalized, the technical evaluation process can then begin. The agent bank should set the ball rolling with a proposal for engaging the economic and legal advisers to assist the pool of participant banks. The first task is for the external auditors to undertake an independent business review (IBR) of the business plan.

The pool of institutions will not act until it has received a favourable report from the IBR. The consultants will review the assumptions made in the financial plan to verify how reasonable these are. They will perform any needed adjustments and evaluate the criteria on which the business is based, including sales forecasts, existence of future orders in the order book and reasonableness of the collection and payment periods, as well as the evolution of various other parameters.

This favourable IBR report can take on particular importance if the restructuring involves the conversion of debt into equity. The value of the new capital contribution is a key element for preventing a loss of profitability for existing and/or new shareholders.

2.4.2 Actions with the banks' technical area

Bilateral negotiations with the members of the pool

Participation in the final loan agreement by each of the members of the pool is one of the most important aspects of the negotiations that are carried out during the restructuring process.

The members with a significant share in the deal will try to include all of the institutions in the operation for the simple reason that if any of the banks were to opt out of the proposed structure, the remaining participants will be required to take on a bigger exposure in the resulting restructuring. The main objective of the principal creditors is to keep the risk assumed within the same levels as originally represented by their share of the initial figure at the time of restructuring.

The subsequent negotiations with each of the members will focus on obtaining agreement for the proposed restructuring from all the members of the pool of participant banks. If any of the institutions are reluctant to participate, the negotiations will focus on the percentage of the unassigned risk to be subscribed to by the other pool members.

Once the final number of participants has been established, the restructuring process will continue through bilateral negotiations focusing now on more specific economic and legal aspects that the institutions will want to impose on the final structure, to be included in the contracts and agreements still to be formalized. These can refer to individual compensations, covenants, special clauses, etc.

Coordination with the agent bank

This point is particularly critical for the ultimate success or failure of the restructuring process. The agent bank will lead the whole negotiation process and run the relations with the pool's economic and legal advisers. It will also work assiduously to bring the operation to a swift and satisfactory conclusion, being aware that the financial position of companies undergoing restructuring could deteriorate over the course of just a few months.

This means that a rapid solution will facilitate the viability of the operation and of the company.

The company must maintain fluid relations with the agent bank, as all the milestones to be reached during the process result from the actions taken on that bank's initiative. Against the backdrop of a crisis like the one we are going through, in which many companies find themselves in the middle of processes of this kind, restructuring departments of financial institutions are swamped with a large number of workouts, making it particularly difficult for them to monitor operations on a timely basis. Any delays affecting the execution of necessary actions may jeopardize the whole restructuring process.

Data room for the associated legal and accounting documentation

The company involved in the restructuring of its liabilities has to prepare all the necessary documentation required by the process. Among those documents are the following:

- Property deeds.
- Deeds and powers of attorney.
- Contracts of various types.
- Financial and business plans.
- Accounts and records of invoices received and sent.

Prior availability of this documentation will facilitate the process of evaluation of the financial plan by the external consultant. Certainly, the sooner the final IBR report is obtained, the more the likelihood of completing the process in a timely manner and successfully.

Subsequently, during the preparation of the contracts, the ready availability of information in the data room will also speed up the conclusion of this phase.

Identification of general and particular guarantees

The structure resulting from the ongoing process must be underwritten by a sufficient quantity of assets to ensure that the loan-to-value (LTV) ratio falls within the range acceptable to the financial institutions.

That is, if a restructuring operation is to be successful, a key element must be the company's capacity to obtain sufficient guarantees to bring to the process, such as, for example, those relating to the number, value and reliability of the assets owned, its capacity to offer mortgage security, its potential to transfer rights on which financial institutions can place a value, and the personal guarantees of the partners that may be executed in the event that the company is unable to provide sufficient security.

Legal review of contract and clauses

The last step before concluding the negotiations and signing the agreements formalizing the restructuring process relates to the legal review of the contracts drafted. The group of participant institutions as well as the company itself will be assisted by legal advisers that will be shouldering the weight of the negotiations at this point. The final result of the bilateral and multilateral negotiations will materialize in the resulting contract; it is vital, therefore, to ensure that it includes all the agreements reached during the negotiations.

Sometimes, even after having reached agreements with the agent bank and the other participants in the process, at the time of putting these agreements down on paper in the contracts new problems may appear; these may arise out of certain legal terms used or specific clauses that each of the institutions may wish to introduce. If the *pari passu* principle is observed, all the institutions must enjoy the same rights and guarantees, and the final document must reflect any clauses demanded by the legal departments of the participant institutions. However, none of them can improve or worsen the relative position of the parties within the syndicated loan.

Final negotiations and signing

All negotiations, individual agreements and contracts produced during the restructuring process lead to the signing of the syndicated loan agreement. This event should be limited to signing the documents and contracts in the presence of a notary, but it is not always incident-free. Last-minute differences that may not always be possible to resolve can arise. These may cause a postponement of the signing until the problems are solved, or even end with the operation being turned down.

Follow-up and monitoring

Once the syndicated loan contract is signed, the agent bank continues with its role of monitoring of and overseeing compliance with covenants and other agreements reached.

After the signing of the loan agreement, the mortgage guarantees provided as security are notarized and registered. This process could be complicated if there were liens or encumbrances on any of the assets. The disbursement of the loan funds is usually subject to compliance with this obligation; if the agent bank does not have the mortgages registered in its name, it will not be in possession of collateral to cover its risks.

2.5 Key points in a process of corporate restructuring

To conclude, let us summarize the key points that should be considered by any company that may be about to embark on a process of financial restructuring:

- Be proactive. Do not propose restructuring as the sole response and the consequence of an upcoming default. Avoid identifying restructuring with de facto default.
- Understand the underlying causes of the liquidity problem and do not just blame others (like, for example, the lack of support from the banks).
- Draw up a consistent and credible action plan to improve the company's liquidity. Determine the financial needs in the short, medium and long-term.
- Be consistent in your financial plan: try to cover short-term needs with short-term funds, and long-term needs with long-term funds. Negotiate your plan following this approach.
- Draw up a negotiating strategy. Put forward arguments to convince the interested parties that the operation is feasible. Foresee the difficulties that will arise in the negotiation process and offer guarantees.
- Do not equate restructuring with debt renegotiation. Long-term needs can and must be financed by converting debt to equity, whenever the level of leverage is excessive.
- When converting debt to equity, negotiate in detail the value of the stake held by the new shareholders or look for alternative sources of capital (venture capital, for example).
- Finally, the success of the restructuring depends to a large extent on the company surrounding itself with qualified advisers who can offer the benefit of their experience in processes of this kind.

2.6 Summary

Corporate financial restructuring involves activities both inside and outside the company. These actions taken within the company basically comprise:

- Defining the liquidity problem: why, how much and when?
- Preparing an internal financial plan, including a short-term treasury plan and a plan for medium- and long-term profitability.
- Determining a strategy for negotiations with the group of banks: what do we offer, to whom and under what conditions?

- Drawing up a preliminary proposal to put to the group of financial institutions.

The external actions involved in a financial restructuring process are aimed at achieving agreements among the parties, by identifying negotiators and possible arbiters, appointing experts for technical and legal matters, and establishing monitoring mechanisms so as to ensure compliance with agreements.

As these external actions are carried out involving the banks, it is worth distinguishing between external actions with the banks' commercial area and external actions with their technical area.

3
Operating Restructuring

3.1 Chapter overview

The objective of any operating restructuring process is to implement operational actions in order to generate a sustainable increase in the Free Cash Flow (FCF). Although we can think about several managerial actions that might temporarily increase the amount of cash, in a restructuring process we should look for a sustainable (permanent) effect. Restructuring is not about a short-term outlook, but a long-term one.

An operating restructuring focused on the generation of new and permanent FCF from operations will try to implement new policies and managerial decisions in relation to the different elements of the Profit and Loss of the company

An operating restructuring focused on the generation of new and permanent FCF from operating working capital should first of all be concerned with minimizing the current assets needed to meet the company's objectives, and thus only finance those resources that are strictly necessary.

From an economic value perspective, all fixed assets should be classified into those that generate value, and those that don't. Keeping this in mind, in any restructuring process all fixed assets should be analysed from this point of view.

3.2 Introduction

The objective of any operating restructuring process is to implement operational actions in order to generate a sustainable increase in the Free Cash Flow (FCF). Although we can think about several managerial actions that might temporarily increase the amount of cash, in a restructuring process we should look for a sustainable (permanent) effect. Restructuring is not about a short-term outlook, but a long-term one.

As we know, the FCF has three components and, consequently, operating restructuring actions can also be differentiated in three categories:

- Actions to increase FCF from operations coming from the P and L.
- Actions to increase FCF from operating working capital (net current assets).
- Actions to increase FCF from investments decisions (Capex).

In this chapter we will discuss some of these actions.

3.3 Increasing cash flow from day-to-day operations

An operating restructuring focused on the generation of new and permanent FCF from operations will try to implement new policies and managerial decisions in relation to the different elements of the company's Profit and Loss. Most operational managers are familiar with this kind of management – that one can call *management thorough P and L* – focused on fixing elements of the P and L: increase of Revenues, control of Operating Costs, reduction of general expenses, and so on.

There are several ways to implement operating restructuring's actions focused on the P and L. For example:

- Redefining the optimal scope of the firm.
- Externalizing processes and downsizing the excess capacity.
- Revisiting the marketing strategy.
- Becoming a global company.
- Changing the operating leverage.

The in-depth analysis and discussion of these management decisions exceeds the scope of this book, which deals with restructuring just from a financial perspective. There is an abundant literature on these topics, including manuals and specialized books.[1]

As a practical example, let's consider the case of the operating leverage.

At the end of the day, any operating restructuring tries to reduce the operational risk of the company, by reducing the volatility of the FCF. How does the management of the P and L might contribute to the stability of the FCF? One way is by implementing that correct level of operating leverage.

Operating leverage is measured by the ratio of fixed costs and fixed expenses in relation to the total costs and expenses of the company. The higher the ratio, the higher the operating leverage. And the higher the operating leverage, the higher the operating risk of the company.

Consider the case of a notional financial company facing two extreme situations (A and B), as shown in Table 3.1.

In situation A the company has only 5% of variable costs, with a higher operating leverage than in situation B, where the company has 75% of variable costs. Note that in both situations operating profitability, measured by the Earnings before Interest and Taxes (EBIT), represents 20% of Revenues.

What happens if the company had a variation of 20% in Revenues?

The EBIT would have a higher volatility in the situation with higher operating leverage. Tables 3.2 and 3.3 show this fact in two different scenarios.

In Table 3.2, an increase of 20% in Revenues leads to an increase in EBIT of 95% in situation A, where in situation B the same variation in Revenues induces an increase in EBIT of 25%.

In Table 3.3, a decrease of 20% in Revenues leads to a decrease in EBIT of 95% in situation A, where in situation B the same variation in Revenues provokes a decrease in EBIT of 25%.

Table 3.1 Initial situation

	% of Revenues	
	Situation A	**Situation B**
	Variable Costs: 5%	**Variable Costs: 75%**
Revenues	100	100
Variable Costs	5	75
Fixed Costs	75	5
EBIT	20	20

Table 3.2 Increase of 20% in revenues

	% of Revenues	
	Situation A	**Situation B**
	Variable Costs: 5%	**Variable Costs: 75%**
Revenues	120	120
Variable Costs	6	90
Fixed Costs	75	5
EBIT	39	25
Variation in EBIT	+95%	+25%

Table 3.3 Decrease of 20% in revenues

	% of Revenues	
	Situation A	**Situation B**
	Variable Costs: 5%	**Variable Costs: 75%**
Revenues	80	80
Variable Costs	4	60
Fixed Costs	75	5
EBIT	1	15
Variation in EBIT	–95%	–25%

This close relationship between operating leverage and volatility reflects some economic realities, like economies of scale for the company and the dilution of fixed expenses in expanding industries.

Establishing an appropriate level of operating leverage is a key factor for taking advantages of these facts, thus linking expectations and stability of future FCF.

3.4 Increasing cash flow from operating working capital

An operating restructuring focused on the generation of new and permanent FCF from operating working capital should first be concerned with minimizing the level of current assets needed to meet the company's objectives, thus limiting the financing only to those resources that are strictly necessary.

The steps involved in managing net current assets should be taken in the following logical order:

- Minimizing the current assets required.
- Managing their financing efficiently.

It should avoid situations in which the company may be required to finance assets in excess of those needed.

It is surprising to see how often in practice this logical order is changed. In many companies there are untapped opportunities for creating economic value by improving the management of current assets, because the fact that assets have a financial cost is often overlooked. In addition, managing these short-term net assets effectively requires monitoring and close control of details which may *prima facie* look unattractive and tend to be delegated to staff with inadequate qualifications for that task.

Operational working capital is made up of short-term assets and liabilities that a company needs as a result of day-to-day operations. In fact, operational working capital is also called Net Current Assets, and it is equal to current assets minus current liabilities.

Properly managed, operational working capital is a source of liquidity and, in the end, of economic value. CFO is a global professional publication that runs annually a survey on the working capital situation for a large number of companies on several continents. It is interesting that this survey consistently shows how the level of working capital kept by companies is much larger than that is considered a prudent one.[2]

Working Capital management is not as glamorous as some other activities of the firm. But the application of best practices here can generate a sustainable flow of wealth. As always, the devil is in the details.

To analyse those operating actions that contribute to generating more FCF from the working capital, let's have a look at the factors that should stand out when defining a policy to manage net current assets in the context of creating value for the company.

3.4.1 Managing accounts receivable and accounts payable

Accounts receivable and accounts payable are a result of the company's commercial policies – policies relating to sales and purchases – regarding its customers and suppliers. Although the supplier–customer relationship is normally managed from a commercial business point of view, it has a number of financial aspects that should not be overlooked. From the supplier's viewpoint, every company needs to consider the following financial aspects of its relationships with its customers:

- Terms of sale.
- Payment instruments.
- Cash from the customer.

Actions on terms of sale

When talking about the terms of sale, it is worth keeping in mind the financial impact of managerial decisions on issues like the actual number of days to collect sales revenues and the applied discounts for early payment.

Any action to reduce permanently the days a company needs to collect its sales is a healthy way to increase the economic value of the company. To begin, the question we must answer is: Do we know the actual days we need to collect our sales?

The actual number of days to collect sales does not usually coincide with the days agreed when setting the terms of sale because, among other reasons, the supplier and customer do not have the same understanding of when the period starts and ends. For the supplier, the actual days to collection start on the date on which the product or service is invoiced and end on the day collection actually takes place. For the customer, this period often starts on the day the product is received, or the day the invoice is accepted, and the end date is that on which the payment order is issued. Experience shows that, depending on the industry in question, the difference between the theoretical and actual days to collection can be considerable. Moreover, if the customer establishes specific monthly payment days, the impact on the supplier can be even greater.

Sometimes, in order to prevent the actual number of days to collection from becoming excessive, companies offer so-called early payment discounts. Although the commercial aspects of this practice are clear, it is important to bear in mind its financial impact. In its simplest version, a discount for early payment is made when the customer decides to pay cash rather than wait for the end of the payment term. In return, the customer receives a sum that is usually calculated as a percentage of the net amount shown on the invoice. This is therefore a financial operation in which the supplier obtains financing at a cost, and the customer invests money for a return. It is important to remember that an early payment discount is a zero-sum game, in which one party's cost represents the other's profit. What is the effective cost of this operation?

Suppose that we establish a commercial relationship between A (supplier) and B (customer) whereby A collects after 120 days. Let's suppose that B takes advantage of an early payment discount, for which it receives 3%. It is commonly said that A is obtaining finance at 9%, which in a scenario in which financing costs 7% would imply it includes a risk premium of 2%. The calculation of the effective cost of financing may differ because, among other things, of the time value of money, which is a consequence of its inherent opportunity cost.

The daily interest on the transaction then becomes:

$$Id = [1/(P - C)] \times [D/(1 - D)]$$

where:

Id = daily interest, expressed as an integer.
P = payment period agreed, in days.
D = discount offered, expressed as an integer.
C = period for cash payment up front, in days.

It is often the case that C isn't zero. And it can be as much as 30 days. If this were the case, the daily interest on this finance for the supplier would be:

$$Id = (1/90) \times (0.03/0.97) = 0.00034364$$

This represents a daily interest rate of 0.034364%.
Its equivalent annual rate (Ia) would be:

$$Ia = (1 + Id)^{365} - 1 = 1.00034364^{365} - 1 = 0.1336$$

This represents an annual interest rate of 13.36%.

In summary, this operation would cost 13.36% if the real period to cash money up front is 30 days instead of 0 days. What had a nominal cost of 9% results in an operation with an effective cost of 13.36%.

As we can see, the transaction turns out very well for the customer, who invests risk free and obtains a return of 13.36%. Again, what is a return for the customer represents a cost for the supplier, who is getting financing at 13.36% and paying a premium of 6.36% (13.36 – 7.00) to ensure its collection, providing the supplier had access to alternative bank financing at a cost of 7%.

Actions on payment instruments

There is a broad spectrum of payment instruments, ranging from negotiable instruments, promissory notes, and commercial bills to cash and cheques. This is another point that must be specified at the outset of any commercial relationship as it could become the cause of delayed payments. From the supplier's point of view, the choice of invoicing method can be made on the basis of a number of factors which are summarized in Table 3.4 below.

Table 3.4 Comparative analysis of payment instruments

Instrument	Initiative	Period	Cost	Key factor
Cheque	Customer	0–2 days	Commissions for other bank	Pay on the day, before a given time
Promissory note	Supplier	0 days	Commissions for collection	Direct debit
Cash	Customer	1 day	No	Pay on the day, before a given time
Cards	Mixed	Depending on presentation	Yes	Mass process

Some comments on the information given in Table 3.4.

- The payment instrument should be negotiated within the framework of the relationship between the supplier and customer, and the choice may sometimes be the indicator of the relative strengths of the parties involved in the relationship.
- The effective cost of each alternative is a combination of the number of days to payment and the commissions negotiated.
- In Table 3.4, 'key factor' represents the main action that the supplier must take into account when deciding on the relative suitability of the instrument being considered.

As already mentioned, the relationship between the supplier and customer is generally viewed as being a zero-sum game, in which a gain for one of the parties always represents a loss to the other. To create sustainable value it is necessary to overcome this perception and instead establish relationships between the parties in which both sides can win.

Bearing this in mind, in recent years a number of business management tools have become available to facilitate cooperation between suppliers and their customers. One of these tools is Reverse Factoring.

Unlike traditional factoring, where a supplier wants to use his receivables to obtain financing, Reverse Factoring (or *Supply Chain Financing*) is a solution initiated by the purchasing party (the customer) to assist his suppliers in obtaining financing at a lower interest rate than what they would normally be offered. But it is also a solution for the customer, since the factor company takes over the management of payments to its suppliers. The terms and conditions under which this service is provided are stated in a reverse factoring contract between the factoring company and the customer. Although this operation takes many forms, Figure 3.1 summarizes the main features graphically.

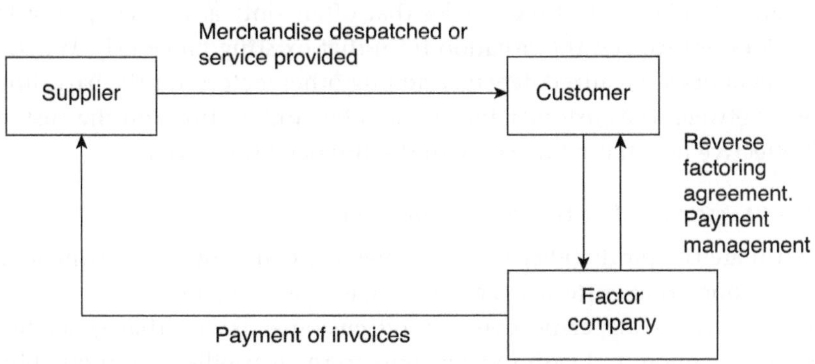

Figure 3.1 Schematic representation of the reverse factoring process

What is original in this business scheme is that it results in a situation in which everyone wins, at least in theory. In effect:

1) The client of the factoring company (purchaser in the sale transaction) receives the following services:
   - Management of payments to suppliers, with the advantage of eliminating the administrative work of a payments department together with cost savings from reduced paperwork, etc.
   - Adoption of the payment method considered most appropriate.
   - Obtaining of alternative finance through the possibility of negotiating new payment periods.
   - The possibility of investing excess liquidity.
2) For the supplier, the reverse factor agreement may represent:
   - The possibility of making direct savings by avoiding costs incurred in traditional methods for collecting payment from customers (stamps, banking charges, etc.)
   - A quick and simple method to obtain financing, thereby complementing bank credit, without a predetermined ceiling since the amount will depend on the invoices accepted by the customer.
   - In some cases, access to financing offered by the confirming or factoring company may constitute an effective transfer of credit, since the financial institution takes over ownership of the credit and the associated risk.
3) For the factoring company (financial institution) this service creates sustainable value, in the sense that it builds the loyalty of existing clients and permits access to new ones, both for lending and deposit transactions.

In short, from the supplier's point of view, reverse factoring can be seen as a means of collection of receivables that offers only advantages, or at the least does not worsen the situation from that existing previously. Whether these benefits are realized depends, among other factors, on the bargaining power between the customer and the supplier and, in turn, on the customer's effective negotiating power with the financial institution.

Actions to estimate the cash generated from the customer

To estimate the profitability of a customer any company must estimate the actual money that customer is generating for the company.

From a financial perspective, a good customer is one that generates a sustainable amount of cash to contribute to the feasibility and profitability of the company. In other words, a good customer is not only one that generates an acceptably high gross margin, but one that generates enough cash flow as well.

Any supplier selling to a customer and not collecting the money on the spot is investing in the customer, that is, financing its operation and assuming a risk. From the supplier's perspective, how should we analyse the reasonable limit of risk to afford in a particular customer? By understanding the economic feasibility of the company in which the supplier is investing: the answer is by assessing the economic feasibility of the customer.

In Chapter 1 we have developed the methodology to make this analysis.

A practical example

The points to consider in the process of improving accounts receivable management can be summarized in the following points:

1) Analysis of the current situation.
2) List of problems detected.
3) Objectives to be met.
4) Envisaged impact on the organization.
5) A list of actions and of persons responsible for those actions.

We will discuss these points with the help of an actual example.

As a part of the process of privatization of state-owned companies in Spain, a well-known Spanish business group considered the suitability of improving its management of receivables. From its analysis of the current situation the following problems were detected:

1) A significant difference existed between the theoretical and real terms of collection.
2) There was no centralized risk policy.
3) Management coordination of receivables collection between the financial and commercial areas was inadequate.
4) The company's information system was not oriented towards providing useful management information and was being used inefficiently.
5) There was an absence of standardized reporting.

This list, which is by no means exhaustive, gives us an idea of the main problems that can hinder the development of a sufficiently effective collection management system. In the case we are concerned with here, for each of the problems identified one or more measures were put in place to solve it or minimize its impact and a schedule for action was defined and the suitable responsible individuals assigned.

For example, when examining the delays in payment by some customers it was found the basic reason was that the company was using a payment modality that either did not suit what customers needed or that they had expressly asked for. The task of matching the means of payment with the type of customer, which was carried out by the billing department over a six-month period, reduced the portfolio of defaulters significantly.

A collections committee was set up to facilitate coordination between the areas involved. Among other measures, a procedure for identifying the causes of delays in payment was put in place, and criteria were established for linking customer payments with sales incentives. In addition, the content of the operating account for type A customers was defined.

Similarly, a Risk Committee was set up in order to produce a uniform classification of customers and establish a single risk limit for each type of customer.

Finally, bonuses were established for meeting the targets for recovering matured customer debt and for reducing the average number of days to collection.

3.4.2 Managing inventories

When designing an inventory management policy the main issues about what decisions are required can be summarized as:

1) The level at which inventory management is going to be carried out.
   Subject to the volume involved, control can be performed at the level of individual articles, families of articles, etc.
2) The type of inventory you want to control.
   Basically, we might be dealing with stocks of raw materials, semi-finished or finished products. On this point it is important to determine whether there is a backup or adjustment stock and to quantify it as accurately as possible.
3) The costs of the stock.
   This is usually identified in terms of the cost of ordering and carrying the stock as well as opportunity cost of the funds tied up in it.
4) The order size and order point.
   This is usually defined via simulation models minimizing the lead time and total cost of inventory, based on a series of forecast assumptions about the projected evolution of variables such as sales.

3.5 Investing wisely

From an economic value perspective, all fixed assets should be classified into those that generate value and those that don't. Keeping this in mind, in any restructuring process all fixed assets should be analysed from this point of view.

The practical consequences of this analysis are clear:

1) For new investments, accept only those that add the highest economic value.
2) For existing investments, proceed to replace those that are not generating the expected economic value.
3) If there is no replacement available, proceed to divest on those investments.

When applying this methodology to real-life situations, a common pitfall is to consider accounting profitability as the reference to make the decision; it is not.

Let's consider the case of Superval, a food distribution company located in Spain. In 2013 the company was analysing the possibility of writing off an old warehouse facility that Superval was not using any more. The facility still had an estimated net accounting value of €500,000, and liquidating the asset would generate likely net cash of only €100,000. The company's management was reluctant to liquidate the asset because the write-off would generate an estimated loss of €400,000 as result.

Assuming that the company had no alternative use for the warehouse, the estimated loss is not the appropriate yardstick against which to measure the impact of the decision. Instead, the differential after taxes cash flow generated is the correct approach. In fact, the proper analysis should include the following steps:

Identification of the realistic alternatives:

Alternative 1: do nothing
Alternative 2: proceed with the write-off

Differential after taxes cash flow associated to the alternatives (assuming a tax rate of 30%):

Alternative 1: Present Value of future tax savings coming from the remaining depreciation[3]
Alternative 2: +€100,000 + 0.3 × €400,000 = €220,000

Accordingly, the relevant criteria is the estimated present value of cash flow (after taxes) associated to the different realistic alternatives the company has. In the present case, the correct decision should be to go ahead with the write-off now.

In general, consider the differential and estimated real money, not only the accounting profit or loss. In the case of any doubt as to whether any given specific economic fact should be included in the analysis of value creation in a given decision, we need to ask if:

1) it's a cash flow, that is, it involves a real payment in or out;
2) it's differential, that is, it only takes place if the decision is made; or
3) it's net of tax, that is, it refers to the situation after the effect of tax has been taken into account.

Only if the answer to all three of these questions is 'yes' should the factor in question be included as a differential cash flow. However, the difficulty tends not to be a conceptual one but a practical one, that is, it is very easy to miss out cash flows that are differential.

To prevent this from happening, it is worth listing a series of rules of thumb applicable to the economic analysis involved in of any decision:

Rule 1

Do not forget the initial outlay and any successive outlays needed to meet working capital requirements as a result of an incremental investment in the working capital.

In fact, many investments in fixed assets result in an increase in the volume of business, thereby causing greater current asset requirements – in terms of customer receivables, inventory and cash in hand – and produce more financing from short-term liabilities – suppliers, creditors, deferred taxes, etc. The net result of these financing requirements and sources of funds is a differential cash flow that must be considered as part of the decision-making process.

Rule 2

Do not overlook the possible final liquidation of the final working capital and/or the liquidation of part of the initial investment.

Any economic analysis occurs in a given time horizon, even in the case where the decision being analysed is intended to have an unlimited duration: it would be a nuisance to have to draw up cash flow forecasts indefinitely. Therefore, there must always be a final year in the analysis, in which the possible liquidation of differential business has to be included, or its residual value estimated.

If it is assumed that the investment is liquidated in the final year, do not forget to include the cash flows it generates, net of tax.

Rule 3

Ignore sunk costs, that is, those costs already paid and which cannot be recouped, unless they have a differential effect on tax liability.

The past does not create economic value, unless it teaches us how to make better decisions.

Rule 4

Differentiate past cash flows from future cash flows.

In other words, forecast properly and do not limit your forecasts to a slavish repetition of the past. It is usually the case that we are preparing a forecast precisely because we want the future to be better or we expect it to be different.

Rule 5

Be systematic about analysing cash flows.

Practice teaches that if you are not systematic it is easy to leave out important elements that may be relevant to the analysis. The FCF definition gives us a systematic procedure for ordering possible differential cash flows.

1) Free Cash Flows from operations.
2) Free Cash Flow arising from the operational working capital requirements.
3) Free Cash Flow arising from investments in, or divestments of, fixed assets.

Rule 6

Do not forget the possible interrelationships among projects. If there are any make sure those can be quantified reasonably well.

In order to establish clearly any possible interrelationships between projects it is essential to define the existing alternatives correctly, both in terms of their financial value and their time horizon. Otherwise it would be easy to fall into a kind of 'analysis paralysis' as, broadly speaking, everything can be related to everything else.

A typical example of an interrelationship is that arising when analysing the creation of value in a project that uses excess capacity. One of the keys to avoiding a common mistake is to have a very clear idea of what the alternative uses might be for this unused capacity, if any, both in the present and the future. And, as a result, you need to be sure of the extent to which this capacity is actually free and when it ceases being unutilized.

Rule 7

Beware of the opportunity cost trap.

Inappropriate use of the concept of opportunity cost is a frequent cause of wrong decisions that destroy value. Opportunity cost must always be defined in the context of the real alternatives available. Postulating unreal or incomplete alternatives can lead to confusion since, at the end of the day, everything may be considered an opportunity cost for something else.

Let us suppose that, as a member of the Investment Committee of your company, you are involved in a decision to be made about whether or not to approve an investment in a new factory. One of the key factors is to ascertain whether this new factory will create economic value. To do so, it will be necessary to include all the right cash flows and to avoid including any unnecessary ones. During the meeting members of the Investment Committee raise the following issues:

The land on which the factory is going to be built belongs to the company and the company has no alternative use for it. Assuming that it is a prime site in an area undergoing industrial expansion could mean that its market value is considerable. Specifically, the book value of the land is €200 million and it could currently be sold for €600 million. This difference of €400 million between the two does not show in the project analysis consideration, but it is a clear fact that it represents a potential loss of income or opportunity cost for the company if the project is approved. As a result, it should be included as a negative cash flow.

In the case in question, this market value is not a cash flow for the project, since in order to convert a market value into cash the land needs to be actually sold, in which case we would not have a factory. Accordingly, selling the land becomes a different investment project, which competes with the one under consideration, on the assumption that there would be an alternative use for one of the assets that the company currently owns. The aim here would therefore be to focus on the value created by each of the mutually exclusive projects and select the best one.

Rule 8

Free Cash Flow (FCF) is the best first step for managers to tackle rather than dismiss operational risk.

Free cash flow is the key entry point. The degree of risk depends on its volatility; and the volatility of FCF is the key to understanding operational risk. As already commented, make a distinction between operational risks as it relates to profit and loss (P and L) and in relation to the balance sheet. In terms of P and L, we are talking mainly about operational risk in relation to revenue, expenses and cost.

Ultimately, we're talking about operational risk related to total net assets. Another critical factor is capital intensity. It's higher when, say, the company needs higher investment to set up a new business unit; that means the volatility of free cash flow is greater.

3.6 Summary

The objective of any operating restructuring process is to implement operational actions in order to generate a sustainable increase in the Free Cash Flow (FCF). Although we can think about several managerial actions that might temporarily increase the amount of cash, in a restructuring process we should look for a sustainable (permanent) effect. Restructuring is not about a short-term outlook, but a long-term one.

An operating restructuring focused on the generation of new and permanent FCF from operations will require the implementation of new policies and managerial decisions in relation to the different elements of the Profit and Loss of the company. Most operational managers are familiar with this kind of management – that we can call *management thorough P and L* – focused on fixing elements of the P and L: increase of Revenues, control of Operating Costs, reduction of general expenses, etc.

An operating restructuring focused on the generation of new and permanent FCF from operating working capital should first of all be concerned with minimizing the current assets needed to meet the company's objectives, and thus, only obtaining financing that is strictly necessary.

Working Capital Management does not have the glamour of other more visible company activities. However, the application of best practices on this issue can lead to the generation of sustainable flow of wealth. As always, the devil is in the details.

To estimate the profitability of a customer a company needs to estimate the real money that the customer is generating for the company.

From a financial perspective, a good customer is one that generates sustainable and sufficient cash to contribute to the feasibility and profitability of the company. In other words, a good customer is not only a customer that generates a good gross margin, but enough cash flow as well.

From an economic value perspective, all fixed assets should be classified into those that generate value and those that don't. Accordingly, in any restructuring process all fixed assets should be analysed with this point of view in mind.

To conclude, any operational restructuring requires analysis, decision-making and management to carry it out. Obviously, as in all management tasks, there is always the alternative of doing nothing. However, this is still a decision, and one that leads to a form of management by default. Experience shows that this kind of decision and this passive style of management are not favourable to the creation of value for any business.

4
Financial Restructuring

4.1 Chapter overview

Any company dealing with a corporate restructuring process has a lot of problems. To solve them it's necessary to understand their nature and causes. Most problems in a company come from the operating aspects, not from the financial ones. Consequently, before trying to set up a permanent financial solution for a company, we need to understand why the company is not generating enough cash and we have to conceive a realistic and doable business plan to address the critical issues. In other words, before trying to finance an operational problem, try to solve it. Financing operating inefficiencies is the best way to end in financial distress.

Financial leverage properly managed is a way to generate economic profitability in a company. Good management entails maintaining the level of debt within certain limits. In this context, one necessary step in any financial restructuring is to determine the debt capacity of the company.

When a company is involved in a corporate restructuring, to determine the debt capacity of that company we need to have reference to the optimal capital structure the company should have.

Having decided the amount of debt and the capital structure associated with the financial restructuring, an additional important point is to select the type of debt to be used.

4.2 Introduction

Any company dealing with a corporate restructuring process faces a lot of problems. To resolve them it's necessary to understand their nature and causes. Most problems in a company originate in the operating side of the firm, not in the financial. Consequently, before settling on a permanent financial solution, we must understand why the company is not able to generate enough cash, and we have to conceive a realistic and feasible business plan that addresses the critical issues. In other words, before trying to finance an operational problem, let's try solving it. Financing continuing operating inefficiencies is the best way to end up in financial distress.

This is common sense, but it's surprising how often we make decisions forgetting this point.

Let's now consider an investment decision. Before thinking how to finance it, let's be sure that the investment is good *per se*, independently of how the investment will be financed.

How can we do this? By estimating the reasonable expected differential Free Cash Flows (FCF) associated with the investment, and by calculating the expected economic profitability (IRR of the FCF). If the expected economic profitability is low, and you believe there is not a reasonable way to change this expected outcome, do not waste your time trying to convince investors to finance that investment. If you don't have conviction about that investment, how could you expect investors to have it?

Financial restructuring actions try to find a permanent solution for a lack of cash, but these actions are never the entire solution for making up for that lack of cash. So, providing we are already working on the causes of insolvency originating from the operational aspects of the company, we must also think about how to improve the generation of cash by introducing changes in the financial policies of the company.[1]

In this chapter we plan to discuss how to do this.

4.3 Actions on debt capacity

Financial leverage properly managed is a way to generate economic profitability in a company. Good management entails maintaining the level of debt within certain limits. In this context, one necessary step in any financial restructuring is to determine the debt capacity of the company.

The debt capacity of a company depends on the right balance between expected FCF and economic feasibility of the company together with the expected profitability for the shareholders.

The higher the amount of debt, the higher the expected profitability for the shareholders, providing the company generates enough FCF to be economically feasible.

In our valuation model based on discounted cash flows, we assume that

Economic Value = Present Value of FCF, discounted at WACC

Since FCFs are independent of the amount of debt, and the higher the debt is, the lower is the WACC, therefore, according to this model, the higher the debt is, the higher the EV would be.

Clearly, the theoretical solution that our valuation model offers is in clear contradiction with business practice,[2] since companies do not base their financing policies on using 100% of debt for their capital structure.

What is missing in the Miller and Modigliani model to give us such an outlandish solution? Does it invalidate the model? Not really, but instead it shows us that in order to apply it to the issue in question we must revise some of its underlying assumptions.

Firstly, our model assumes that a firm's operating leverage is independent of the level of debt. From this viewpoint, the FCF would be entirely independent from the level of debt the company had to manage. This assumption, which may be reasonable if we assume marginal variations in the level of debt in the capital structure, is not at all reasonable if the financial leverage increases substantially. In practice, it results that the FCF is not independent of the level of debt above a certain degree of leverage.

Some reasons for this are:

1) Additional costs may emerge associated with the option of bankruptcy, which alters the operating cash flows. For example, the so-called 'underinvestment effect', whereby the firm's managers would not undertake profitable investments either because almost all of the potential value generated would go to the creditors, or conversely they may lack the resources to make that investment. Similarly, the firm's operating flows would be affected by the potential loss of confidence among its commercial creditors, or by the reduction in the operating value of existing assets due to its maintenance expenses being reduced to the minimum.[3]
2) There is a loss of management effectiveness, which must focus on managing the debt.
3) Excessive debt sends a negative signal to the market.
4) Agency costs increase as a result of conflicts of interest between managers, shareholders and creditors.
5) Experience shows that there exist patterns of discrimination between sources of financing to cover investment needs that tend to protect the

value of existing shareholders against that of potential new shareholders, thus limiting the entry of new shareholders[4] and potentially limiting the scope for new investments.

The theoretical economic valuation model built using Miller and Modigliani's hypothesis and the CAPM model assumes that operating risk remains constant for all levels of debt. This leads to a theoretical solution in which the optimal financial structure is to use 100% debt. To resolve this inconsistency we must introduce the concept of negative value of the direct and indirect costs of debt[5] (i.e. bankruptcy costs) into the economic value.

Accordingly,

$$EV = PV\ (FCF, WACC) - PV\ \text{Cost associated to debt or bankruptcy costs}$$

For small variations in the amount of debt, bankruptcy costs remain very low. But if the company increases its amount of debt above a reasonable limit, the theoretical decrease in EV in response to the reduction of the WACC is lower than the increase in the costs of bankruptcy, with the economic value of the company going down accordingly.

Figure 4.1 shows some estimated distress costs by industries.

Our research shows that companies with a preponderance of intangible assets are most vulnerable to financial distress. Knowledge-intensive industries such as high technology and life sciences lose up to 80% of enterprise value in times of financial distress, while tangible-asset companies, like those in petroleum and railroads, lose as little as 10% on average.

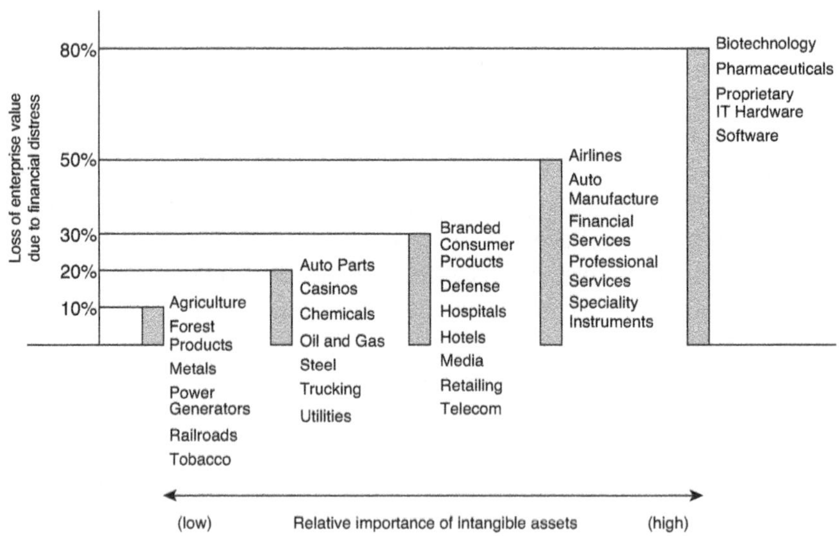

Figure 4.1 The impact of distress costs by industry

Source: Harvard Business Review.

In practice, how do companies manage their financing decisions so that this effect is included in the cost of debt and they can decide on the right capital structure? What criteria do they use for deciding whether to finance new projects with long-term debt or equity?

4.3.1 An example of debt capacity

Let's consider the example of Optima, S.L. and assume that the firm's managers are analysing whether or not to invest in a project called 'Globix'. After a detailed study is completed, the operational characteristics of the project can be summarized as shown in Table 4.1.

Table 4.1 Expected operational assumptions, Globix project

1. Time horizon:	5 years				
2. Assumptions about operational cash flows:					
Years	1	2	3	4	5
Sales (000 of €)	1,500	1,575	1,670	1,720	1,376
Cost of sales (% of sales)	60%	59%	58%	58%	58%
Operating Expenses (% of sales)	20%	20%	19%	19%	19%
Depreciation of Fixed Assets:					
Depreciation Methods			linear		
Depreciation period with accounting criteria			7 years		
Depreciation period with technical criteria			5 years		
Depreciation period with fiscal criteria			8 years		
Tax rate			30%		
3. Assumptions about cash flows from operational working capital:					
Initial investment in Operational WC expected evolution in Operational WC components:			100 thousand euros		
Years	1	2	3	4	5
Account receivables (days of sales)	60	60	58	57	55
Inventories (days of CoGS)	30	28	27	26	25
Account payables (days of CoGS)	75	75	75	75	75
Liquidation value of Operational WC last year					60%
4. Assumptions on cash flows related to investments in Fixed Assets:					
Initial investment			600 thousand euros		
Annual investment in maintenance			80 thousand euros		
Liquidation value last year			20 thousand euros		

Prior to financing any project, it is a good idea to ensure that what we are investing in is a good business venture, independently from how we plan to finance it.

In this case, before considering how to finance the Globix project, it is worth ensuring that it is a good investment. To do so, we proceed to calculate the IRR of the expected FCF.

According to the projections, the future operating cash flows will be:

Expected FCF: Figures in 000 euros

1. Operational Cash Flows: Figures in 000 euros

Years	1	2	3	4	5
Sales	1,500	1,575	1,670	1,720	1,376
Cost of sales	900	929	968	997	798
Gross margin	600	646	701	722	578
Operating expenses	300	315	317	327	261
Depreciation expenses	75	90	105	120	135
EBIT	225	241	279	276	181
Taxes	68	72	84	83	54
EBIaT	158	169	195	193	127
Operational Cash Flow	233	259	300	313	262

This is due to the fact that the depreciation charges will vary as follows:

Evolution of Depreciation Expenses: Figures in 000 euros

Years	0	1	2	3	4	5
Base to depreciation		600	720	840	960	1080
Depreciation coefficient		0.125	0.125	0.125	0.125	0.125
Depreciation Expenses		600	646	701	722	578

since differential depreciation is that calculated using tax criteria.

The cash flows from managing net current assets are as follows:

2. Cash Flows from Operational WC

Years	0	1	2	3	4	5
Initial investment	–100					
Evolution on balances						
Acc. Receivables		247	259	265	269	207
Inventories		74	71	71	71	55
Acc. Paybles		185	191	199	205	164
Total		136	139	138	135	98
Variation in Operational WC		–36	–4	1	3	37
Liquidation						59
Tax saving due to loss						12
Total CF on Operational WC	–100	–36	–4	1	3	107

This includes the liquidation of assets in the fifth year, net of taxes.

Finally, the cash flows associated with investments in fixed assets are as follows:

3. Cash Flows from invest in FA						
Years	**0**	**1**	**2**	**3**	**4**	**5**
Initial investment	−600					
Investment maintenance		−120	−120	−120	−120	−120
Liquidation value						20
Tax saving due to loss						197
Total CF from Inv FA	−600	−120	−120	−120	−120	97

And the tax saving for the liquidation in year 5 is:

Tax shield due to liquidation:	
Gross Fixed Assets (book value)	1,200
Accumm. Depreciation	−525
Net Fixed Assets (book value)	675
Liquidation value	20
Loss due to liquidation	655
Tax saving	197

As a result, the FCF associated with the Globix project may be summarized as follows:

Expected FCF: Figures in 000 euros						
Years	**0**	**1**	**2**	**3**	**4**	**5**
CE from Operat		233	259	300	313	262
CF from Operat WC	−100	−36	−4	1	3	107
CF from Inv FA	−600	−120	−120	−120	−120	97
FCF	−700	77	135	182	196	466

And the resulting IRR of these FCFs is 11.7%.

Having verified that the investment is profitable, we need to consider how to finance it. At this stage we need to consider the following:

1) Whenever it's possible and appropriate, priority should be given to debt, since it is a cheaper source of funds.
2) The possibility of using debt depends on how feasible the project is.
3) The convenience of using debt depends on factors relating to the profitability of the project and its impact on the firm as a whole.

Let us apply these ideas to our example firm, Optima, S.L.

We know that the Globix project is a good investment and the firm's current capital structure is 30% debt. Could this project be financed with a larger percentage of debt? Provided that the FCF generated allows the debt commitments to be met, the answer is yes.

Let us now analyse what would happen if we financed the project with an initial loan equivalent to 40% of the investment, carrying an interest rate of 5% p.a. and repayable in annual instalments of €56,000 over five years.

The projected debt service would be:

Debt evolution

Years	0	1	2	3	4	5
Debt	280	224	168	112	56	0
Interest Expenses		14	11	8	6	3

The estimated Free Cash Flow for Shareholders or Equity Cash Flow (ECF) would be:

Estimated Equity Cash Flow

Years	0	1	2	3	4	5
FCF	–700	77	135	182	196	466
Debt repayments	280	–56	–56	–56	–56	–56
Interest(1–t)		–10	–8	–6	–4	–2
ECF	–420	11	71	120	136	408

The resulting profitability for shareholders (IRR of ECF) is 15.2% due to the type of financing associated with the project. Remember that if there was no debt, the expected profitability would be 11.7%

Even though using this 40% of debt is theoretically possible, the ECF for the first two years are very small, meaning that any negative deviation from the forecasts could jeopardize the feasibility of the project, requiring, as a result, an injection of liquidity from shareholders.

In order to analyse the different alternatives for the financing of the Globix project, we can summarize various scenarios that produce different rates of return and risks of illiquidity, as shown in Table 4.2.

According to this analysis, the Globix project could be financed with an initial 40% of debt component, at 5% p.a. interest and constant annual repayments over five years of €56,000 each.

Table 4.2 Summary of scenarios

Scenarios	1	2	3	4	5	6
Initial level of debt	50%	40%	30%	20%	10%	0%
Equity Cash Flow 1st year (€'000)	–5	11	28	44	60	77
Return to shareholders	16.6%	15.2%	14.1%	13.2%	12.4%	11.7%

Nonetheless, what is possible is not always necessarily the most advisable course of action. How, then, can we discern what would be an appropriate level of debt?

As mentioned earlier when analysing the feasibility of the Globix project, the first criterion is to achieve the right balance between the return that shareholders demand and the risk of illiquidity. On the one hand, while financing the project with 40% of debt is theoretically possible, it is certainly not very advisable, unless one is absolutely certain of the cash flow from the project. On the other hand, financing it with 10% of debt will make life much easier for the managers, but at the price of lower returns for shareholders. This would generate a conflict of interests between the managers and shareholders, which is a manifestation of what is known as 'agency costs'. In order to strike the right balance between these opposing interests, it is necessary to consider factors such as how predictable the cash flows associated with the project are and the risk profile of the managers who are going to run it.[6]

However, all the financing decisions associated with a specific project need to be analysed in the context of the company's general business plan. Thus, the suitability of a given level of debt for the Globix project depends on Optima, S.L. having other investment projects available in the future. In practice, companies take these interrelations into account by considering criteria such as the following:

1) **Flexibility.** This may be important, since financing Globix with debt may lead to the loss of future investment possibilities, as a result of a lack of outside finance. If flexibility is important, greater emphasis should be placed in using equity.
2) **Control.** By contrast, the criterion of keeping ownership control would lead to financing the project with debt in order to prevent the dilution of ownership that would result from issuing new shares. One way of resolving the apparent contradiction between flexibility and control is by using hybrid financing instruments such as convertible bonds, which make it possible to keep control at the start without sacrificing future

flexibility. This approach also avoids dilution of ownership when the bonds are converted, provided the projects financed in this way generate economic value.

3) **Dilution of earnings per share (EPS).** Dilution of earnings per share is sometimes said to be a crucial factor in financing decisions. On this view, by diluting EPS, the share price will drop. Thus, given that raising finance by issuing shares dilutes EPS, preference should be given to using debt.

   To what extent is avoiding dilution of EPS important? Is it a criterion that should be taken into account when deciding on how to finance business projects? As with all financial or accounting metrics, maintaining EPS has relative importance to the extent that what is important is not that EPS is diluted, but failing to understand the causes for its dilution. Accordingly, we need to distinguish between the immediate and indirect causes for the EPS dilution, since all financing that requires an increase in capital invariably produces an immediate dilution of EPS. This, in turn, in the medium to long-term may result in an increase in EPS (mediate dilution) assuming that the investment project generates economic value. In any case, a dilution of EPS, even when it is immediate, should be accompanied by an explanation of its reasons and those actions that will enable the value creation to be re-established.

   Applying the above criterion to the case of the Globix project, the management of Optima, S.L. should explain that it is investing in a highly profitable project, and that is using equity to finance it. It could be that, for example, it has a portfolio of future projects in which it may be important to keep open the option of resorting to debt as the preferred financing instrument. This would lead to value creation which is compatible with the short-term dilution that could otherwise occur.

4) **Expectations.** Another important criterion when deciding to finance a business venture concerns the expectations that exist about the future of the company and the progress of the financial markets and the markets in which the company operates. Indeed, Optima, S.L. could justify the use of its own resources for this project by indicating that any new projects would be financed with debt. By doing this, Optima is not just keeping open those financing alternatives, but it may be also anticipating a downward trend in future interest rates.

5) **Risk.** As mentioned earlier, the perceived and real risk in the projects (i.e. operating risk) as well as the company's current structure of financing

(financial risk) are important criteria for deciding how to choose the financing for an investment. In general, it could be said that given similar levels of risk, those projects with lower levels of operating risk will favour a greater use of debt. By contrast, for projects with similar levels of operating risk the company should choose equity if it considers that its current level of financial leverage is excessive.

6) **Comparison with other companies.** Benchmarking against the capital structure of peer companies is a common criterion used to decide on project financing. As happens with all comparative decision criteria, it would be wise to err on the side of caution, depending on the specific case in question. For example, what constitutes a comparable company usually will depend on the goals being pursued. Comparable companies are not necessarily those in the same sector. In some cases, it is a better criterion to use a similar level of operational risk.

Assuming that these criteria were considered in the case of the Globix project and the company we are discussing, the situation is as follows:

- Optima, S.L. had a capital structure comprising around 30% debt.
- The company's management considered that this structure should be maintained in the future.
- The Globix project was not a one-off project for Optima, S.L., but formed part of an approved investments plan.
- In this context, it was decided that it was important to retain the flexibility for taking on more debt in the future to finance new investments.
- Although the Globix project would have allowed more debt to be taken on, it was decided that it should be financed with an initial 30% debt, through a five year loan with the following terms (in thousands of euros):

Debt evolution						
Years	**0**	**1**	**2**	**3**	**4**	**5**
Debt	210	168	126	84	42	0
Interest Expenses		11	8	6	4	2

The company financed the project with €490,000 of equity that resulted in an estimated profitability for its shareholders of 14.1%, as shown in Table 4.3.

Table 4.3 Estimated equity cash flow

Years	0	1	2	3	4	5
FCF	-700	77	135	182	196	466
Debt repayments	210	-42	-42	-42	-42	-42
Interest (1–t)		-7	-6	-4	-3	-1
ECF	-490	28	87	135	151	422
IRR	14.10%					

4.4 Actions on capital structure

When a company is involved in a corporate restructuring, in order to determine its debt capacity we need to have reference to the optimal capital structure that is suitable for the company. How are we able to estimate its optimal capital structure?

As stated previously, we know that:

EV = PV (FCF, WACC) – PV Cost associated to debt or bankruptcy costs

Any company facing a corporate restructuring increases its EV by permanently increasing its FCFs as a result of the actions involved in operating restructuring. But what happens if the company changes its amount of debt? By changing the amount of debt, the company will be changing its EV because of the resulting changes in its WACC and in the bankruptcy costs. For small variations in its debt outstanding, these bankruptcy costs (bc) remain very low. But if the company increases its debt above a reasonable limit, the resulting theoretical increase in EV due to a reduced WACC becomes lower than the increase in the bc and the company's economic value goes down as a consequence.

Accordingly, for any company that faces a corporate restructuring, the optimal amount of debt is one in which the marginal increase in EV resulting from a reduction in its WACC is equal to the marginal decrease in EV due to the increase in bc. At that level of debt, the EV of the company reaches its highest level because it includes the larger impact in economic value coming from the operating as well as the financial restructuring.

Let's next consider the case of Marquis Inc., a Canadian company involved in a corporate restructuring. After implementing all the expected operating actions in the restructuring process, the Free Cash Flows would be:

Years	1	2	3	4	5
FCF after operational restructuring	200	250	275	300	325
Terminal Value					1,625
FCF total	200	250	275	300	1,950

The company has a present capital structure of 20% of debt. How can we be sure that 20% debt results in a reasonable capital structure to be considered as part of its financial restructuring? One way is by analysing the optimal capital structure that Marquis can have after the restructuring process.

To do this, we have to estimate the expected evolution of the cost of debt for Marquis associated to different levels of financial leverage. Assuming an unleveraged beta of 0.8, a tax rate of 30%, a risk free (Rf) rate of 5% and a market premium (MP) of 4%, we estimate the evolution of the WACC associated to different financial leverage to be as follows:

Debt	20%	25%	30%	35%	40%
Equity	80%	75%	70%	65%	60%
Beta u	0.8	0.8	0.8	0.8	0.8
Rf	5.0%	5.0%	5.0%	5.0%	5.0%
MP	4.0%	4.0%	4.0%	4.0%	4.0%
Ke,u	8.2%	8.2%	8.2%	8.2%	8.2%
Kd	6.0%	6.0%	6.5%	6.5%	6.8%
Ke,l	8.75%	8.93%	8.93%	9.12%	9.17%
WACC	7.84%	7.75%	7.62%	7.52%	7.39%

Certainly, the EV of Marquis, Inc. will change according to the different capital structures considered. Assuming some estimated bankruptcy cost,[7] we can project the optimal capital structure for the restructured company, considering that the financial leverage will maximize the economic value of the company:

Debt	20%	25%	30%	35%	40%
Equity	80%	75%	70%	65%	60%
EV without bc	2,178.5	2,185.9	2,197.1	2,205.2	2,215.9
Marginal variation in EV		7.4	11.2	8.1	10.7
Bankruptcy costs	200.0	204.0	210.0	218.1	235.0
Marginal variation in BC		4.0	6.0	8.1	16.9
EV with bc	1,978.5	1,981.9	1,987.1	1,987.1	1,980.9

As shown above, the optimal capital structure of Marquis should be approximately at 35% of debt, a level where the marginal increase in the EV due to a lower WACC equals the marginal reduction in the EV associated with the change in bankruptcy costs.

In Appendix 1 we develop a more detailed explanation.

4.5 Actions on the type of debt

Having decided the amount of debt and the capital structure associated with the financial restructuring, another important point to keep in mind is the selection of type of debt to be incurred.

There are some golden rules on this topic. Let's discuss some of them.

Always finance short-term needs with short-term financing instruments, and long-term needs with long-term financing instruments.

As an example, let's consider the case of Cortefiel's acquisition by two Private Equity Firms (PAI/Permira and CVC) in July 2005.

Cortefiel was a Spanish textile company operating in several countries. Its main line of business consisted of selling clothes at the retail level through an extensive chain of retail outlets operating under different commercial names (Cortefiel, Springfield, Pedro del Hierro, Douglas, Milano, Don Algodón and Women's Secret). At the end of February 2005, the company had 1,100 sales outlets in 37 countries and employed a total of more than 8,500 people. Over 90% of the company's sales outlets were owned by the Group, with franchises occupying an almost marginal position for the company.

The acquisition of Cortefiel was financed through a highly leveraged capital structure operation. After negotiating with a number of financial institutions, CVC reached agreements for the following financing plan (figures in millions of Euros):

Uses of finance	
Purchase of shares	1,400
Repayment of existing debt	38
Cost of the operation	44
Total uses	1,482
Sources of finance	
Capital	388
Senior debt	671
Mezzanine debt	273
Bridging loan for the sale of buildings	150
Total sources	1,482

The senior debt was structured in three tranches with the following characteristics:

	€m	Initial cost	Duration	Repayment
Senior A	337	2.25%	7 years	Repayment plan
Senior B	167	2.75%	8 years	Bullet loan
Senior C	167	3.25%	9 years	Bullet loan

The mezzanine debt was structured over 10 years, with an initial cost of 10.5% with a single repayment at the end of the loan (i.e. a bullet loan).

A bridging loan was repaid at the end of the first year, with an interest cost of 2.25%.

As we can see, the acquisition was financed, as it should be, using long-term financing to cover long-term investments, and short-term financing to cover a short-term period in which the new Cortefiel would implement the sale of some buildings.[8]

4.5.1 Synchronize the timing of debt servicing with that of the expected FCF.

The restructuring actions on the operating side of the business should generate an expected FCF for the company. The timing for debt servicing included in the financial restructuring should be consistent with the timing of these expected FCF.

This is a crucial point in some cases because one of the covenants explicitly included in most loan contracts is the fulfilment of some conditions for the interest coverage ratio of the debt (RCSD). This RCSD is the ratio between generated FCF and total service of the debt, and some covenants may establish that this ratio must be higher than, for example, 1.5 times on a yearly basis.

Returning now to the acquisition of Cortefiel in 2005, this operation included an operating restructuring that materialized in a business plan for the company. This business plan for the next five years was basically as follows:

- Increasing sales by 38% over the next five years, through a policy of opening a number of new stores and maintaining revenue levels at the existing stores.
- Improving gross margins by 2% of sales, as a result of substantially increasing purchasing in lower cost Asian countries. Although the company had begun to relocate its sourcing and production to Asia

in recent years the plan envisaged for the next five years needed to be more ambitious. It was anticipated that the 2% improvement would be achieved gradually over the first two years.

- Taking advantage of the distinct opportunities to cut costs in the operating expenses front, in view that its overheads stood at eighty million Euros and could be optimized. As with all family firms, some of these expenses included payments that represented indirect remuneration for family members and could therefore be easily eliminated as result of the reorganization.
- The business plan envisaged an improvement in the management of the company's operating working capital. Cortefiel was operating with a stock rotation rate that was well below the standard for the industry, which was around 3 times a year. Moreover, it would also be desirable to shorten the time taken to collect payment from customers.
- Finally, an investment of 153 million Euros in new store openings was envisaged over the next five years. The company also planned an average annual investment of 26 million Euros in maintenance, computer systems, and other items.

The implementation of this business plan would generate a FCF that can be summarized as follows:

Years	1	2	3	4	5
Operating cash flow	133,843	138,677	149,326	158,867	167,057
Cash flow from working cap	–5,765	–7,115	–10,010	3,270	18,893
WC for FA invest/divest	128,809	–56,700	–56,400	–55,200	–53,700
FCF	256,887	74,862	82,916	106,937	132,250

Now, we can compare these FCF with the evolution of the service of the debt associated with the financial restructuring of the new Cortefiel:

Years	1	2	3	4	5
FCF	256,887	74,862	82,916	106,937	132,250
Interest × (1–t)	–37,161	–34,652	–34,211	–33,329	–32,237
Amortization of debt	–157,000	–21,000	–42,000	–52,000	–65,000
Equity Cash Flow	62,725	19,210	6,705	21,608	35,013

In this case, the expected evolution of the RCSD would be:

Year	1	2	3	4	5
RCSD	1.32	1.35	1.09	1.25	1.36

4.5.2 Use the most suitable debt instruments

Keeping in mind the previous points, in most cases the analysis of financial slack and/or flexibility is a key point in determining what type of borrowing instrument to choose.

Companies with high growth opportunities tend to be more conservative in their capital structure and pay more importance to flexibility, since they would not want to lose future investment opportunities for the lack of financing.

The value of a company (EV) can be broken down in two components: the Basic EV (the EV associated with a continuing scenario), and the Growth Opportunities EV (the EV resulting from future and new opportunities for growth):

EV of a company = Basic EV + Growth Opportunities EV

As the EV of the company mainly comes from the second of these components, it should prioritize flexibility at the top by setting up a more conservative capital structure and using debt instruments that allow higher liquidity.

As an example, let's consider the case of Discasa, a company in the food distribution business and operating in the Canary Islands, Spain. Its growth started to slow down since 2005 due to:

- Firstly, a serious threat of competition started to arrive in the Islands through supermarket chains such as Superdiplo, and major chain stores such as Mercadona, Alcampo, Carrefour and others. Up to that point, the geographical location of the Canary Islands had been, to some degree, an entry barrier for competitors wishing to penetrate into that market.
- Secondly, it was difficult to maintain growth within the Islands by opening new establishments, since most areas of commercial interest were already covered, and new openings could only result in a 'cannibalization' among the existing supermarkets.

At the beginning of 2007, facing the different alternatives the company had, the management team decided that Discasa was an effective company, well managed, and with an efficient system that could be transferred to other distribution companies located elsewhere in the Iberian Peninsula. Accordingly, they chose to continue with their growth plan outside the Canary Islands and expanded into the Iberian Peninsula, becoming in the end a major player in the food distribution industry.

The first step in this expansion process was in 2008 when Discasa had the opportunity to acquire a company called Suarsa, located in Zaragoza (Spain) with a network of eighty establishments spread throughout the Spanish autonomous regions of Aragón, La Rioja and Navarre.

To finance this operation, Discasa considered the following alternatives:

1) External financing through a private issue of non-convertible bonds. They were not inclined to issue convertible bonds since shareholdings were already quite well split among various shareholders.
2) Raise private capital to increase equity. There were several options:
   - Make the offer only to existing shareholders. This was unfeasible due their lack of interest.
   - Open the offer to new investors. A financial entity had informally confirmed its interest for participating in the capital increase with the intention of buying Suarsa.
   - A mixed financing, combining capital increases with external financing.

The acquisition of Suarsa was an important initial step but not the only one. Assuming they were successful in this operation, the company should continue with the expansion process in the Spanish mainland by making new purchases, and it should not take longer than two or three years to make a new one. These factors had an impact on the financing plan with respect to the purchase of Suarsa. Although the acquisition could be financed only with bonds, Discasa's management team decided to go for mixed financing via new capital and bonds, in order not to lose the necessary flexibility to take advantage of future new acquisition opportunities.

4.6 Some common financing errors

If a company does have operating problems, making changes only in the financing is never the solution to them. In the face of operating problems, we need operating solutions, not *magical* financial solutions. But the situation can become even worse if the management of the troubled company makes errors in the financing.

One of these common errors is trying to take advantage of asymmetric information that exists among the different stakeholders of the company. Lack of transparency is never a good policy.

Consider the case of Pescanova, a leading group in the food industry. Founded in 1960, the company gambled on vertical integration, which went from catching their products, through their processing up to obtain the targeted final product, to their establishment in the main markets in Europe, America and Japan. Within this vertical integration, the initial access to the resources was obtained by catching them with its fishing fleet or farming them in its various farms.

At the beginning of 2013, the Pescanova Group included more than 160 companies. The company was present in five continents and in more than twenty countries. It had its own fleet with more than 100 vessels, about 50 fish-farming plants, and more than 30 processing plants where it processed more than 70 marine species, selling its products under 16 trademarks of its own. Its workforce reached approximately 10,000 people.

Facing the normal problems associated with the decrease in consumption as a result of the economic crisis that started in 2007, by 2013 Pescanova was not generating enough FCF to cover its debt service payments and it started to renegotiate the terms of external financing it had with its creditors. Its external auditors at that time (BDO) refused to issue an opinion on the financial statements presented by Pescanova, on the grounds that it lacked transparency about the real amount of its outstanding debt. The new external auditors (KPMG) conducted a forensic audit trying to clarify the number of companies in the group and the actual amount of debt. The amount reported changed from €1,522 million, in September 2012, to more than €3,000 million. Since 15 March 2013 the company has been suspended from listing at the Madrid Stock Exchange. After a major confrontation at its Board of Directors meeting in July 2013, Pescanova's President was fired. In September 2013 the shareholders nominated a new President with the mandate to restructure Pescanova.

4.7 Summary

Any company dealing with a corporate restructuring process faces a lot of problems. To solve them it is first necessary to understand their nature and causes. Most problems in a company come from the operating side of the business, not from the financial side. Consequently, before attempting to arrive at a permanent financial solution, we need to understand why the company is not generating enough cash and what realistic business plan we have to address the critical issues. In short, before addressing an operational problem with financing, let's try to solve the operational problem itself. Financing operating inefficiencies is an assured road to financial distress.

Financial leverage properly managed is a way to generate economic profitability in a company. Good management entails maintaining the level of debt within certain limits. In this context, one crucial necessary step in any financial restructuring strategy is determining the debt capacity of the company.

When a company is involved in a corporate restructuring, to determine the debt capacity of that company we need to have reference to the optimal capital structure the company should have.

Having decided the amount of debt and the capital structure associated with the financial restructuring, an additional important point is to select the type of debt to be used.

On this topic, there are some golden rules, like the following:

- Finance short-term needs only with short-term financing instruments, and long-term needs only with long-term financing instruments.
- Synchronize the timing of the service of the debt with the timing of the expected FCF.
- Use the most appropriate debt instrument.

If a company does have operating problems, making changes only in the financing is never the solution to them. In the face of operating problems, we need operating solutions, not *magical* financial solutions. But the situation can become even worse if the management of the troubled company makes errors in the financing.

One of these common errors is trying to take advantage of asymmetric information that exists among the different stakeholders of the company. Lack of transparency is never a good policy.

Appendix

Appendix 4.1: Some bibliographical references on Optimal Capital Structure

Ahn, D., Figlewski, S. and Gao, B. (1998), 'The Adaptive Mesh Model: A New Approach to Efficient Option Pricing', Discussion Paper, New York University Stern School of Business.

Altman, E.I. (1984), 'A Further Empirical Investigation of the Bankruptcy Cost Question', *The Journal of Finance*, 39, 4, 1067–1089.

Andrade, G. and Kaplan, S. (1998), 'How Costly is Financial Distress (not Economic)? Evidence from Highly Leveraged Transactions that Became Distressed', *The Journal of Finance*, 23, 5, 1443–1493.

Black, F. and Cox, J. (1976), 'Valuing Corporate Securities: Some Effects of Bond Indenture Provisions', *The Journal of Finance*, 31, 2, 351–367.

Black, F. and Scholes, M. (1973), 'The Pricing of Options and Corporate Liabilities', *Journal of Political Economy*, 81, 3, 637–654.

Boyle, P. and Lau, S. (1994), 'Bumping Up against the Barrier with the Binomial Method', *Journal of Derivatives,* 1 (4), 6–14.

Brennan, M.J. and Schwartz, E.S. (1978), 'Corporate Income Taxes and the Problem of Optimal Capital Structure', *The Journal of Business,* 51, Jan., 103–114.

___ (1980), 'Analyzing Convertible Bonds', *Journal of Financial and Quantitative Analysis,* 15, 907–929.

Cannaday, R. and Yang, T. (1996), 'Optimal Leverage Strategy: Capital Structure in Real Estate Investments', *Journal of Real Estate Finance and Economics,* 13, 263–271.

Cheuk, T. and Vorst, T. (1996), 'Complex Barrier Options', *The Journal of Derivatives,* 4, 8–22.

Ciochetti, B. (2004), 'Loss Characteristics of Commercial Mortgage Foreclosures'.

Ciochetti, B., Deng, Y., Lee, G., Shilling, J. and Yao, R. (2003), 'A Proportional Hazard Model of Commercial Mortgage Default with Originator Bias', *Journal of Real Estate Finance and Economics,* 27, 1, 5–23.

Cohen, R.D. (2001), 'An Analytical Process for Generating the WACC Curve and Locating the Optimal Capital Structure'. http://rdcohen.www.6.50megs.com/abstract.htm.

Damodaran, A. (2001), *Applied Corporate Finance,* John Wiley Finance, New York.

Derman, E., Kani, I., Ergener, D. and Bardhan, I. (1995), 'Enhanced Numerical Methods for Options with Barriers', *Goldman Sachs Quantitative Strategies Research Notes.*

Fourt, R., Matysiak, G. and Gardner, A. (2006), 'Capturing UK Real Estate Volatility', Paper presented at the 13th Annual European Real Estate Society (ERES) Conference, Weimar, Germany.

Fou, Q., LaCour-Little, M. and Vandell, K. (2003), 'Commercial Mortgage Prepayments under Heterogeneous Prepayment Penalty Structures', *Journal of Real Estate Research,* 25, 3, 15–37.

Gau, G. and Wang, K. (1990), 'Capital Structure Decisions in Real Estate Investment', *Journal of American Real Estate and Urban Economics Association,* 18, 4, 501–521.

Graham, J. (2000), 'How big are the Tax Benefits of Debt?', *Journal of Finance,* 55, 5, 1901–1941.

Graham, J. and Harvey, C. (2002), 'How do CFOs make Capital Budgeting and Capital Structure Decisions?', *Journal of Applied Corporate Finance,* 15, 1, 8–22.

Haug, E.G. (1998), *The Complete Option Pricing Formulas,* McGraw Hill.

Hull, J.C. (2003), *Options, Futures and Other Derivatives,* (5th ed.), Prentice Hall.

Kraus, A. and Litzenberger, R.H (1973), 'A State Preference Model of Optimal Financial Leverage', *Journal of Finance,* 28, 4, 911–922.

Kamrad, B. and Ritchken, P. (1991), 'Multinomial Approximating Models for Options with k State Variables', *Management Science,* 37 (12), 1640–1652.

Kane, A., Markus, A.J. and Mc Donald, R.L. (1984), 'How Big is the Tax Advantage to Debt?', *Journal of Finance,* 39, 3, 841–853.

___ (1985), 'Debt policy and the Rate of Return Premium to Leverage', *Journal of Financial and Quantitative Analysis,* 20, 4, 479–499.

Leland, H. (1994), 'Corporate Debt Value, Bond Covenants, and Optimal Capital Structure', *Journal of Finance,* 49, 4, 1213–1252.

Leland, H. and Toft, K.B. (1996), 'Optimal Capital Structure, Endogenous Bankruptcy, and the Term Structure of Credit Spreads', *Journal of Finance,* 51, 3, 987–1019.

Longstaff, F. and Schwartz, E. (1995), 'A Simple Approach to Valuing Risky Fixed and Floating Rate Debt', *Journal of Finance*, 50, 3, 789–821.

Lintner, J. (1965), 'Security Prices, Risk, and Maximal Gains from Diversification', *Journal of Finance*, 20, 4, 587–615.

Merton, R.C. (1974), 'On the Pricing of Corporate Debt: The Risk Structure of Interest Rates', *Journal of Finance*, 29, 2, 449–470.

____ (1977), 'On the Pricing of Contingent Claims and the Modigliani-Miller Theorem.', *Journal of Financial Economics*, 5, 241–249.

____ (1991), *Continuous Time Finance*, Blackwell.

Modigliani, F. and Miller, M. (1958), 'The Cost of Capital, Corporation Finance and the Theory of Investment', *American Economic Review*, June, 261–297.

____ (1963), 'Corporate Income Taxes and the Cost of Capital: A Correction', *American Economic Review*, June, 433–443.

Ritchken, P. (1995), 'On Pricing Barrier Options', *The Journal of Derivatives*, 3, 2, 19–28.

Sharpe, W.F. (1964), 'Capital Asset Prices: A Theory of Market Equilibrium Under Conditions of Risk', *Journal of Finance*, 19, 3, 425–442.

The European Group of Valuers' Association (2000), 'European Valuation Standards 2000', (4th ed.), Estates Gazette.

Titman, S. and Torous, W. (1989), 'Valuing Commercial Mortgages: An Empirical Investigation of the Contingent Claims Approach to Pricing Risky Debt', *Journal of Finance*, 44, 2, 345–373.

Titman, S., Tompaidis, S. and Tsyplakov, S. (2004), 'Determinants of Credit Spreads in Commercial Mortgages', Working Paper.

Trigeorgis, L. (1993), 'The Nature of Option Interactions and the Valuation of Investments with Multiple Real Options', *Journal of Financial and Quantitative Analysis*, 28, 1, 1–20.

Vandell, K., Barnes, W., Hartzell, D., Kraft, D. and Wendt, W. (1993), 'Commercial Mortgage Defaults: Proportional Hazards Using Individual Loan Histories', *Journal of American Real Estate and Urban Economics Association.*

5
Valuation in Distress

5.1 Chapter overview

In crisis situations gauging the economic value of a company's assets plays a key role in deciding whether to persevere with a business or not. A company is considered to be in distress when it is unable to meet debt payments, often following failed attempts to generate the necessary cash flow by implementing operational restructuring measures.

In order to reach a debt restructuring agreement through a private procedure it is first necessary to do a valuation of the company. It is therefore a question of agreeing on a valuation in which the banks accept that they would be better off being creditors of the restructured firm (the value of their stake being the debt) than being creditors of a company that is not going to be restructured (i.e. the liquidation value of the firm).

The economic value of the company in liquidation will obviously be the value it can obtain from the sale of all its net assets after tax. It is therefore a market value from which the applicable tax must be deducted.

5.2 Introduction

In crisis situations, estimating the economic value of a company's assets plays a key role in deciding whether to persevere with a business or not.

This issue is currently under the spotlight, attracting interest beyond just the academic. Bear in mind that valuation in distress is one of the biggest difficulties that countries now face in their ongoing struggle to implement repeated reforms in their finance systems. Moreover, it has become obvious that there is little hope of emerging from the current economic situation unless the financial systems in affected countries have been reformed.

A company is considered to be in distress when it is unable to meet maturing debt payments, often following failed attempts to generate the necessary cash flow by implementing operational restructuring measures.

When a company is in distress, it faces two options.

1) Reach an agreement on debt restructuring through private proceedings.
2) File for insolvency which could result in an insolvency agreement or in liquidation.

In order to reach a debt restructuring agreement through private proceedings it is first necessary to perform a valuation of the company.

It is therefore a question of agreeing on a valuation in which the banks accept that they would be better off remaining as creditors of the restructured firm (the value of their stake being the debt) than being creditors of a company that is not going to be restructured (i.e. the liquidation value of the firm).

5.3 How to evaluate a company in distress

The key to carrying out a reasonable valuation lies in establishing the main objectives that the valuation process needs to achieve.

It is important to remember that:

1) The value that you need to establish is the company's economic value, not its accounting value, sentimental value, literary value or any other kind of value that is not a true economic value.
2) The overriding aim is to establish the economic value of the company's net assets.[1]
3) The economic value can be the extrinsic value,[2] which is quantified by means of external or market references, or the intrinsic value,[3] which is based on the fundamentals of the business set out in its business plan.

The economic value of the company in liquidation will clearly be the value that can be obtained from the sale of all its net assets after tax. It is therefore a market value from which the applicable tax must be deducted.

Valuing the company as if unlevered is a good starting point because it allows comparison of the (unlevered) going concern value (economic value of the operating firm) with a liquidation value of the assets. Such a comparison will show us if carrying out a financial restructuring is worth it. There are examples in lots of markets where the liquidation value of tangible assets is higher than the going concern value of the firm. In such a case, liquidating the firm will probably be the option preferred by financial creditors. Conversely, should the going concern value result be clearly higher than the liquidation value, the firm's financial creditors might well decide considering alternative financial restructuring options.

What is the best way to determine the reasonable value of a company if it chooses the debt restructuring option?

In theory, it doesn't seem reasonable to confine the analysis to only one extrinsic value reference, given that it is a question of estimating the economic value that will result from a restructuring. It is more logical to define exactly what the restructuring process will consist of, ensuring that it includes both operating and financial restructuring components, valuing the company in a scenario in which such changes have already been implemented with due consideration given to what is the firm's sensitivity to those variables that affect its economic value. In fact, this exercise is an excellent tool that enables us to uncover all key restructuring drivers and how and when it becomes advisable to implement value- maximizing strategies.

For this type of valuation it is usually a good idea to use the discounted cash flow method, and compare the value obtained with market references.

Could it make sense to value the firm by considering real options? The answer is yes, provided that these options have a clear economic value, which means that they must be exclusive and explicit. In any case a valuation based on real options should be similar to valuations made using discounted cash flows, including the possible value of operating flexibility.

Table 5.1 shows the key elements that must be considered when carrying out a valuation of a company in distress.

In short, in order to estimate the value of the restructured company it is necessary to estimate the Free Cash Flows (FCF) which would result from managing operating assets if the restructuring plan were to go ahead, and then discount these flows at the weighted average cost of capital (WACC)

Table 5.1 Key elements in valuation

Value of the company in liquidation	⟹	Market value (after tax)
Value of the restructured company	⟹	Define restructuring plan: Operating Financial
		Intrinsic value based on the business plan: PV (FCF, WACC)

associated with these FCF and with the new capital structure defined as a result of the restructuring process.[4]

Note that this method produces an estimated value of the company's operating assets. If the company in distress has non-operating assets and the operating restructuring plan doesn't make provisions for their use, it will be necessary to make the pertinent adjustments (positive and negative) in order to include the value that could be derived from said operating assets.

Finally, by comparing the estimated value of the restructured firm (economic value of the total net assets) with the value of the debt in the restructured company, it is possible to estimate the economic value of the company's own resources.

Let's apply these concepts to a real case.

5.4 An example of valuation in distress

Let's consider the case of the company Grove Inc.

At the end of 2014, Grove Inc. had a serious liquidity problem as a consequence of a decrease in revenues and higher operational costs and expenses. The company was unable to generate enough cash flow to cover its short-term operational and financial payments. Moreover, in the last years the situations of the markets had provoked an important decline in the market value of some strategic assets of the company, reducing the value of some of the collateral associated to its long-term financing.

Grove Inc. faced a situation of economic distress and was in the process of negotiating a private agreement with a pool of banks to change the present terms and conditions of the debt, to make the company viable again. At the end of the day, this agreement would determine how to distribute the expected future cash flow generated by Grove among the various commercial and financial creditors, thus avoiding bankruptcy and/or liquidation, situations from where most of its participants will come out with economic losses.

The company had to implement an operational and financial restructuring plan, looking for a fair balance between survival and sacrifices to be asked from the different economic agents involved in the operation: financial entities, shareholders, and stakeholders (customers, employees, etc.).

A summary of the balance sheet of Grove Inc. at the end of 2014 was as follows (figures in millions of euros):

Operational Current Assets	200	Operational Current Liabilities	100
		Debts with Financial Entities	650
Net Fixed Assets	500	Equity	–50
Total Assets	700	Liabilities + Equity	700

As already mentioned, the situation the company faced was unsustainable and the new owners and management of Grove started negotiations with the financial entities, in order to set up a restructuring plan. Part of this negotiation process was to get refinancing from the banks by convincing them that the value of Grove in liquidation was lower than the value of Grove after implementing the restructuring. In other words, the banks had to agree that if they liquidated the company now the resulting losses would be higher than the losses they had to afford as a result of the restructuring process.

5.4.1 The liquidation value of Grove Inc.

Consequently, a first objective was to reach an agreement on the liquidation value of the company now, based on the figures shown in the balance sheet and on the situation of the market.

Liquidation value of Net Current Assets	20
Liquidation value of Net Fixed Assets	200
Total liquidation value of Net Assets	220
Total Debts	650
Total expected losses from the liquidation (after taxes)	430

The liquidation value after taxes of the Total Net Assets of Grove was follows (in millions of euros):

These liquidation values were a consequence of the Spanish real estate situation at the end of 2014, that included losses resulting from the liquidation of current operating assets and current liabilities.

5.4.2 Valuation of Grove Inc. after implementing the restructuring plan

During the last months of 2014, the new management team of Grove developed a new business plan for the company, with the following improvement objectives included in its operational aspects:

a) In relation to FCF from Operational P&L:
   Expected Revenues for first year (2015) would be €600 million, with a Gross Margin of 40% and operational expenses of 20%. Expected Depreciation would be 5% of Revenues and marginal tax rate would be 20% on earnings. These operational ratios would remain in the next 4 years, for a total time horizon of 5 years, and Revenues would increase 5% every year.

b) In relation to FCF from Operational Working Capital:
The introduction of better practices in the management of operational working capital would lead to a reduction in the Operational Current Assets from 150 days of sales, in 2015, to 140 days in 2016; 135 days in 2017; 130 days in 2018; and 125 days in 2019.
Operational Current Liabilities would be half the amount of Operational Current Assets yearly.

c) In relation to FCF from Capex:
The restructuring plan of Grove included an investment plan in Fixed Assets with the following calendar and amounts:

Years	**2015**	**2016**	**2017**	**2018**	**2019**
Investments	–200	–100	–50	–69	–73

The resulting total expected FCF coming from the restructuring plan is shown in Table 5.2.

Based on expected FCFs, the management team of Grove Inc. negotiated a new financing plan with the financial entities. According to this, the banks accepted a recapitalization of an amount of €250 million (conversion of debt into capital), and the shareholders invested €100 million in new capital to contribute to the reduction of the debt.

The liabilities of the company changed accordingly, as detailed in Table 5.3.

Based on this new capital structure, Grove Inc. would need to incur additional new debt in the coming years in order to fulfil its operational business plan, assuming that all the positive FCFs generated in the next five years

Table 5.2 Expected FCFs (Figures in million euros)

Years	**2015**	**2016**	**2017**	**2018**	**2019**
FCF	–123	10	61	47	50

Table 5.3 Changes in the liabilities of Grove, Inc.

	Initial	**Conversion of debt into capital**	**New capital**	**Final**
Operational Current Liabilities	100			100
Debts with Financial Entities	650	–250	–100	300
Equity	–50	250	100	300
Liabilities + Equity	700			700

would be exclusively dedicated to cover the service of the debt (payments of interest expenses and amortization of the principal).

Appendix 5.1 shows a detailed numerical explanation of the expected evolution of Grove's financial statements for the next five years.

Assuming an average cost of debt of 6%, Table 5.4 shows the expected evolution of Grove's debt after the restructuring.

Table 5.4 Expected evolution of BS

Expected evolution of BS	Initial after restructure	2015	2016	2017	2018	2019
Net Current Assets	100	125	123	124	125	127
Net Fixed Assets	500	670	739	755	790	827
Total Net Assets	600	795	861	879	916	953
Debt	300	437	449	409	382	350
Equity	300	358	412	470	534	603
Total D + E	600	795	861	879	916	953

The expected evolution of the company's capital structure at accounting value would be:

	Initial after restructure	2015	2016	2017	2018	2019
Debt	50%	55%	52%	47%	42%	37%
Equity	50%	45%	48%	53%	58%	63%

Why would the financial entities involved accept this financial restructuring, under the assumption that they agree on the operational restructuring? It is simply because the liquidation value of Grove now (€220 million) is lower than the value of the debt after the restructuring (€300 million); the banks are now owners of a company which is supposedly sustainable from the economic point of view, since it is both feasible and profitable.

In fact, the expected profitability for the banks as owners of the restructured company will depend on the economic value of the restructured Grove and on the participation of the ownership the banks will now have in the conversion of the firm's debt into capital.

Appendix 5.2 includes a numerical explanation of the valuation of Grove, assuming that the resulting operational and financial restructuring is implemented.

With a reasonable terminal value of Grove in 2019,[5] the Enterprise Value (EV) of the restructured Grove is €607 million, a very similar value to its accounting value. The expected evolution of the capital structure at economic value of the company would be:

	Initial after estructure	2015	2016	2017	2018	2019
Debt	300	437	449	409	382	350
Equity	307	344	383	428	480	542
EV	607	781	832	837	862	892
Debt	49%	56%	54%	49%	44%	39%
Equity	51%	44%	46%	51%	56%	61%
EV	100%	100%	100%	100%	100%	100%

5.5 What about the distribution of economic value?

Summarizing, Grove Inc. will be economically feasible and sustainable if:

1) The new management team is able to implement the operational improvements included in the business plan.
2) These operational improvements will avoid operational losses resulting from the liquidation of operational working capital and fixed assets.
3) The shareholders will invest €100 million in capital to repay debts.
4) Financial institutions will become shareholders of Grove by accepting a recapitalization of the company of €250 million (conversion of debt into capital); in addition, they will keep an additional amount of new debt with a peak of €450 million in 2016.

Providing that with this restructuring the company becomes economically feasible, the next step is to determine the expected economic profitability for the shareholders that will depend on the total value of the company and the value of its participation in the Equity.

As already mentioned, the expected economic value of Grove is €607 million. If the financial entities decide to liquidate the company now, they will get an estimated €220 million plus non-recoverable losses estimated at €430 million.

If banks accept the restructuring, they will then become shareholders and creditors of the company. As creditors, banks will obtain an economic profitability of 6%, which is equal to the estimated cost of the debt.

The new shareholders will be now the banks and the previous shareholders, that contributed to the new Equity with €250 million and €100 million, respectively. Table 5.5 summarizes the associated economic

Table 5.5 Summary of shareholders' profitability

Scenario 1	
Participation of old shareholders	100%
Participation of banks	0%
Profitability for old shareholders	40%
Profitability for banks	0%
Non-recoverable losses for banks	250 million euros
Scenario 2	
Participation of old shareholders	50%
Participation of banks	50%
Profitability for old shareholders	22%
Profitability for banks	2%
Non-recoverable losses for banks	100 million euros
Scenario 3	
Participation of old shareholders	38%
Participation of banks	62%
Profitability for old shareholders	16%
Profitability for banks	6%
Non-recoverable losses for banks	64 million euros
Scenario 4	
Participation of old shareholders	29%
Participation of banks	71%
Profitability for old shareholders	9%
Profitability for banks	9%
Non-recoverable losses for banks	35.7 million euros

profitability for the new shareholders under the restructuring scenario for Grove. Logically, this expected profitability depends on their participation in the new Equity.

The scenarios described in Table 5.5 help us to understand how difficult it is to reach a fair balance among the participants in a restructuring process, in order to share fairly the sacrifices needed to rescue the company.

Under Scenario 1 all profitability will go to the old shareholders, which is an extreme and unreasonable situation.

Scenario 4 shows an apparently more fair situation, since the participation of the players (old shareholders and Banks) is similar to their contribution in money. Nevertheless, the expected profitability for the old shareholders would be very close to their expected minimum return (cost of equity).

Scenario 2 shows an equal participation (50/50) resulting in a very unequal profitability for the different parties.

Perhaps scenario 3 is the most appropriate to reach an agreement on the property for the restructured company, since banks would get a profitability similar to the one they already have as creditors (6%) and the old shareholders would obtain an expected profitability of 16%, or 4% in excess to the cost of capital, estimated at 12%. The associated loss for the banks would be around 26%.

In this case a scenario with no losses for the banks is not reasonable, since then the expected profitability for the old shareholders would be negative (around –2%).

Again, note that here we are dealing with the economic profitability for the shareholders (IRR of expected FCF for shareholders), and not with their accounting profitability (average ROE).[6]

5.6 Some conclusions about the valuation of Grove, Inc.

At the beginning of the previous section we summarized some of the conditions assumed to be implemented in order to transform the company Grove Inc. into a feasible and profitable business.

Let's now complement those conditions with some others, like that:

1) The new management team is able to implement the operational improvements included in the business plan.
2) The resulting operational improvements will avoid operational losses coming from the liquidation of operational working capital and fixed assets
3) The shareholders will invest €100 million in capital to repay debts.
4) Financial institutions will become shareholders of Grove by accepting a recapitalization of the company of €250 million (conversion of debt into capital), and that they will keep an additional amount of debt with a peak of €450 million in 2016.
5) After restructuring Grove Inc. would have an EV of €607 million, a value similar to its accounting value; the expected liquidation value of Grove is lower than the value of the Debt after restructuring.
6) An agreement can eventually be reached on the ownership of the restructured company; in one plausible scenario banks would get a profitability similar to the one they already obtain as creditors (6%) and the old shareholders would gain an expected profitability of 16%, higher than the cost of capital (estimated in 12%). The associated loss for the banks would be around 26%.

5.7 Summary

Let's now summarize the main points of this chapter.

1) Under crisis situations, estimating the economic value of a company's assets plays a key role in deciding whether to persevere with a business or not.
2) A company is considered to be in distress when it is unable to meet maturing debt payments, often following failed attempts to generate the necessary cash flow by implementing operational restructuring measures.
3) In order to reach a debt restructuring agreement through a private procedure it is first necessary to perform a valuation of the company.
4) At the end, it is therefore a question of agreeing on a valuation in which the banks accept that they would be better off being creditors of the restructured firm (the value of their stake being the debt) than remaining as creditors of a company that is not going to be restructured (i.e. the liquidation value of the firm).
5) The key to carrying out a reasonable valuation lies in first establishing the main objectives that the valuation process needs to achieve. This is particularly important for determining the reasonable value of a company in a situation of economic distress.
6) The economic value of the company in liquidation will obviously be the value it can obtain from the sale of all its net assets after taxes. It is therefore a market value from which the applicable tax must be deducted.
7) To estimate the value of the restructured company it is necessary to estimate the Free Cash Flows (FCF) that would result from managing its operating assets if the restructuring plan were to go ahead, and then discount these flows at the weighted average cost of capital (WACC) associated with these FCF and the new capital structure defined during the restructuring process.
8) This method produces an estimated value of the company's operating assets. If the company in distress has non-operating assets and the operating restructuring plan doesn't make any provisions for their use, it will be necessary to make the pertinent adjustments (positive and negative) in order to include the value that could be derived from said operating assets.
9) Providing that under this restructuring the company will be economically feasible, the next step is to determine the expected economic profitability for its shareholders which will depend on the total value of the company and the value of its participation in the Equity.

10) The different scenarios that can be used in the negotiation process help in understanding how difficult it may be to reach a fair balance among the participants in a restructuring process, in order to share equally the sacrifices needed to save the company.
11) And, overall, we have to consider the economic profitability for the shareholders (IRR of expected FCF for shareholders), and not just their accounting profitability (average ROE).

Appendices

Appendix 5.1

Years	2015	2016	2017	2018	2019
Revenues	600	630	662	695	729
Operating costs	–360	–378	–397	–417	–438
Gross margin	240	252	265	278	292
Expenses	–120	–126	–132	–139	–146
Depreciation	–30	–32	–33	–35	–36
EBIT	90	95	99	104	109
Financial expenses	–18	–26	–27	–25	–23
EBT	72	68	72	80	86
Taxes	–14	–14	–14	–16	–17
Net Earnings	58	55	58	64	69

Appendix 5.2

Years	Initial after restructure	2015	2016	2017	2018	2019
Debt	300	437	449	409	382	350
Equity	307	344	383	428	480	542
EV	607	781	832	837	862	892
Debt	49%	56%	54%	49%	44%	39%
Equity	51%	44%	46%	51%	56%	61%
EV	100%	100%	100%	100%	100%	100%
Kd		6%	6%	6%	6%	6%
Rf		5%	5%	5%	5%	5%
PM		5%	5%	5%	5%	5%
Be, l	1.40	1.43	1.28	1.32	1.44	1.57
Be, u		0.81	0.81	0.81	0.81	0.81
Bd		0.20	0.20	0.20	0.20	0.20
Ke, l		12.1%	11.4%	11.6%	12.2%	12.8%
WACC		8.5%	7.7%	7.9%	8.6%	9.3%
Fac desc		1.085	1.169	1.262	1.370	1.497
PV of FCF		–113	8	48	34	33
TV						892
PV of TV						596
PV of Total FCF		–113	8	48	34	629
EV	607					

6
Some Examples of Restructuring (I)

6.1 Introduction

In this chapter we will review some real life examples of restructuring processes in different companies, operating in different industries and dealing with different circumstances. In our analysis we will try to clarify why these companies were running short of cash and what actions were implemented in order to fix the situation.

6.2 Restructuring at Famosa

Toward the end of fiscal year 2009,[1] José de la Gándara decided that the company Famosa,[2] of which he had been appointed CEO a few months before, was facing a critical situation that would determine its future existence.

The onset of the financial crisis in 2007 had reduced sales and narrowed margins, and the company registered losses in the three years comprising the period 2007–2009. Forecasts for the end of the year signalled bankruptcy as the company's shareholders' equity would be in the red.

José de la Gándara was aware that, in addition to the recurring problem of liquidity brought on by the seasonal nature of its sales, the company also had to deal with waning profitability and added financial pressure due to its high financial leveraging and its inability to meet scheduled debt payments (distress).

Mr de la Gándara thought, 'If we expect to survive this, we're going to have to work out a process of financial restructuring. What can we offer financial institutions in order to continue counting on their support?'

6.2.1 Information on the company and the industry

Established in 1957, Famosa was one of the leaders of the toy sector in Spain. It designed, developed and distributed three types of products:

- Dolls
- Plush toys
- Battery-powered vehicles and outdoor toys.

The company added this last line of products to its portfolio as a result of its 2007 acquisition of a rival company (Feber).

A series of characteristics defined the peculiar nature of the toy industry in Spain at that time:

1) Highly seasonal sales. Typically, 70% of full-year sales were concentrated in the last three months (October to December).
2) Greatly dependent on fashion trends, with design playing a key role. Each year, 30–40% of the company's portfolio was revised.
3) Over a year's time went into the planning of each item. In September, the samples and new items would be chosen for December of the following year.
4) Although sales were highly seasonal, the companies' activities were much more regular, with regard to production costs and expenses. These circumstances brought about peaks in short-term needs for cash which were covered with suitably matched debt-based financing.

Toward the end of 2009, Famosa was operating in over 50 countries, with half of sales taking place in Spain. The company's dolls and plush toys were manufactured in China, and its battery-powered vehicles and outdoor toys were produced at its Alicante (Spain) plant.

Several generations of Spanish boys and girls had grown up with Famosa toys, and some of the company's products benefited from nearly universal recognition (dolls such as Nenuco, Nancy and Barriguitas).[3]

6.2.2 The situation in 2009

In early 2009, the company began to face serious problems of liquidity and high financial leverage due to the following:

1) Two leveraged acquisitions that took place at the beginning and in the middle of the period 2000–2010.
2) The wholly debt-financed acquisition of rival Feber in 2007 (battery-powered vehicles and outdoor toys).

3) Significant needs of financing working capital, of a highly seasonal nature.
4) Deterioration of credit markets and thin liquidity in the credit system.
5) Waning consumer demand and deterioration of the market and sales.

Appendix 6.1 contains financial and accounting information on Famosa.

In the opinion of the company's CEO:

> In early 2009, Famosa was facing a situation that was frankly discouraging. Our leverage amounted to nearly 90% of net sales and EBITDA was clearly insufficient. Banks began to turn their backs, refusing us short-term financing precisely when our seasonal performance had given rise to peak cash requirements. In such circumstances, losing short-term financing meant failure.

After studying the situation, management decided that there were only two alternatives:

1) Initiate bankruptcy proceedings that would culminate in one of three possible outcomes: an insolvency agreement, a distress sale or liquidation.
2) Initiate a process of restructuring of the company's debt in order to balance its accounts and make it viable for a subsequent sale.

After considering the proposed alternatives, senior management opted for refinancing its debt. It was estimated that the company would offer relatively scant value in the event of liquidation and that any attempt to sell the company under distress would meet with failure or would bring on considerable destruction of value for creditors and shareholders.

6.2.3 The restructuring

As CEO of Famosa, José de la Gándara was responsible for coordinating management's efforts to restructure the debt in terms that would be accepted by the financial institutions and would allow for a possible future sale of the company at a reasonable price.

By early 2010, Mr de la Gándara had defined a restructuring process based on the following:

1) Short-term financing needs totalling approximately 11 million euros, to be met with a fresh cash contribution of around 11 million euros. Super-senior ranking of debt with regard to guarantees and cost.

2) Rescheduling of existing debt (approximately 110 million euros), with the conversion of around 32.5 million euros to a capitalized syndicated loan (participating loan).
3) Design of a new financing structure, including incentives for long-term debt holders.

A successful restructuring of the company's debt would bring on changes in its balance sheet, as detailed in Table 6.1.

Mr de la Gándara believed that the restructuring process would make the liquidation of the company unwarranted as it would provide a new capital structure more in line with its sector standard of a 55–60% gearing ratio.

He was also aware that, in order to reach an agreement with financial institutions, it would be necessary to offer a credible method of achieving viability and profitability, including a reasonable period of time during which the company could be sold at an acceptable price.

The creditor banks would decide to save Famosa only if they were convinced that its value as a viably operative company was greater than its liquidation value.

Upon discussing this situation with management, Mr de la Gándara pointed out the following:

> Being poor may be our salvation. What I mean is that banks stand to gain very little at this time from the liquidation of Famosa. This will

Table 6.1 Balance sheet prior to restructuring and in pro forma terms after restructuring (Figures in million euros)

	2009	Adjustments	2009PF
Fixed assets	96.3	0.0	96.3
Net working capital	12.1	0.0	12.1
Cash and cash equivalents	0.0	11.1	11.1
Total assets	**108.4**	**11.1**	**119.4**
Shareholders' equity	**–2.6**	**32.5**	**29.9**
Equity	–2.6	0.0	–2.6
Capitalized Syndicated Loan (Participating Loan)	0.0	32.5	32.5
Long- and short-term financial debt	**110.2**	**–21.5**	**88.8**
Syndicated debt	110.2	–32.5	77.7
New lines of liquidity – super-senior	0.0	11.1	11.1
Other debt	0.8	0.0	0.8
Total liabilities and equity	**108.4**	**11.1**	**119.4**

make it easier to convince them that our company is worth more as a functioning firm guided by a coherent business plan than a series of liquidated assets.

6.2.4 The business plan

In April, May and June 2009, Famosa management worked on a business plan based on the company's new strategy. The new focus consisted primarily of the following:

1) Famosa would be transformed from a Spanish exporter to a Spain-based international firm with a global market.
2) Growth in sales would be achieved through the redesigning and updating of the company's historically best-selling classic toys, particularly its line of dolls. Rather than bringing out toys that had not been previously associated with the company, it would update and relaunch its classic products.
3) The whole of the manufacturing of dolls and plush toys would be transferred to China, and battery-powered vehicles and outdoor toys (Feber) would continue to be manufactured at the Alicante (Spain) plant.
4) The new approach also took into account the fact that the Feber line of products had fared worse from the economic crisis than the rest of Famosa's products.

The company unveiled its new business plan in July 2009. Appendix 6.2 summarizes the estimated operating results.

Table 6.2 shows the estimated required investment in working capital and fixed assets for subsequent years.

On the basis of the company's applicable tax rate of 30%, management calculated the future Free Cash Flows resulting from the new business plan.

6.2.5 Selling the new plan

With the newly calculated data and forecasts in hand, management sought to negotiate with financial institutions in July. The outcome of the talks

Table 6.2 Expected evolution of WC and Capex (In millions of euros)

Years	2010	2011	2012	2013	2014	2015	2016
Capex	−5.7	−5.3	−5.1	−5.1	−5.2	−5.3	−5.0
Investment in working capital	−0.1	−0.4	−0.5	−0.2	−0.3	−0.4	−0.4

would be the collaboration of said institutions in the projected restructuring of debt and the emergence of more favourable conditions that would allow the company to remain in business.

The following are the financial expenses associated with the three types of debt:

New super-senior credit line	6.5%
Syndicated debt	6.5%
Capitalized syndicated loan	8.0%

The capitalized syndicated loan would not be amortized and its interest would be capitalized until the sale of the company. The capitalization would increase the carrying amount of the shareholders' equity.

In charge of the negotiation, Mr de la Gándara wondered what line of reasoning could be put forth in order to create a future scenario in which all parties would come out ahead. To this end, he was aware that, in the initial years, all Free Cash Flow would have to be dedicated to cover the service of the debt (financial expenses and amortization of the principal).

Specifically, he believed that negotiations should concentrate on the following issues:

1) Would projected Free Cash Flow (FCF) be enough to ensure the viability and profitability of the company?
2) What should be done with the FCF? Should all of it be put toward debt servicing?
3) What would be a reasonable terminal or sale value at the end of the sixth year (2016)?
4) What profitability could be offered to the financial institutions as new shareholders?

Summarizing the circumstances of Famosa in July 2009, upon commencing negotiation with the pool of banks, Mr de la Gándara stated:

> We must offer banks a solid line of reasoning. Companies are not brought to their knees by their profit and loss accounts, but rather by their cash flows.

6.2.6 Comments on the restructuring

This example allows us to analyse the main characteristics of the restructuring process, and to discuss the outcome that might guarantee the continuity of the company.

In order to reach an agreement on the new financing for Famosa, the management team had to set up and sell a new strategic approach based on the following:

1) Internationalization. Globalization.
2) Focus on existing product lines and activities by updating products.
3) Outsourcing of production.
4) Greater relevance of dolls and plush toys.

In short, the company proposed to tap new markets worldwide while focusing on its historical know-how.

The business plan implies conservative estimated sales growth (3.6% a year on average). Margins would be broadened through the reduction of expenses and the improvement of production efficiency, without excluding required investment.

It seems consistent and thorough.

Appendix 6.3 shows the detailed estimated FCF associated with this business plan.

Based on this analysis, in the event that the restructuring allows the company to continue operating and that it is able to meet the targets of its business plan, we could assume that by selling the company at accounting value in 2016, the economic profitability for the new shareholders (financial institutions) would be over 14%. We can consider this scenario as a minimum in terms of expected profitability, since it seems reasonable to assume that Famosa would be sold in 2016 with goodwill in the sale price.

Obviously, in order to avoid liquidation and generate economic value for the new shareholders, the company will have to generate estimated Free Cash Flows. Even in a conservative scenario in which all of its Free Cash Flows are dedicated to the service of the debt, it would be reasonable to estimate a minimum shareholder profitability of around 14%. A perhaps more likely scenario (TV = 5 times EBITDA) would provide a profitability above 23%.

6.3 Fixing a failed project finance: the case of Autopistas Radiales

In late spring 2009, Osvaldo Martínez, Finance Manager (CFO) at Autopistas Radiales (AR), a private company operating a toll road bypass in Madrid, was analysing with growing concern the drop in revenues and operating earnings the company was experiencing as a result of the reduced traffic on its toll road. In 2008, overall freeway traffic in Spain fell by 12%, quite similar to the drop in traffic the company had, and the trend did not suggest any improvement in 2009. Martínez found the decline both surprising and unexpected, as variations in traffic had traditionally been related only marginally to variations in GDP. Moreover, the drop in toll road traffic in other countries had been more moderate. Appendix 6.4 provides some historical macroeconomic information about Spain.

Martínez worried about the financial situation of Autopistas Radiales (AR), since the company was not generating enough cash flow to meet all its debt payments, due to the fall in revenues. Martínez summarized the situation in the following terms:

> Financial institutions want to renegotiate our debts in terms of costs and amortization schedule, but our present shareholders are trying to avoid changes in the debt conditions. In my opinion, the project needs operational and financial improvements to be economically feasible and profitable. I wonder what options AR has to survive in the face of a crisis like this, apart from trying to sell the project to new owners?

6.3.1 The AR project

Autopistas Radiales (AR) was founded in 2004 in Madrid with the purpose of building and operating a toll road under a 20-year concession from the Spanish central government. The toll road was built as an alternative route to provide a fast exit to the north of Madrid, especially for periods with heavy traffic (i.e. weekends and holidays). Tolls were agreed upon with the Spanish Government in the concession contract. Table 6.3 summarizes the main features of the project.

The AR shareholders were the private companies that either participated in the construction of the freeway (Infraestructuras del Futuro and Coinfrasa) or in its operation (Infravest).

The forecast of total initial investment was around €60 million euros, broken down as detailed in Table 6.4 (figures in euros).

Initial project finance was obtained through a temporary corporate finance agreement in the form of a credit facility from a pool of banks. This would be converted into project finance at the start of 2009. Somewhat simplified, the project's financial structure was as presented in Table 6.5.

This financing was obtained after long negotiations with several banks, based on the figures in the business plan drawn up when the company was founded. This agreement was open for revision in 2009.

Table 6.3 Main features of the Autopistas Radiales project

General details	
Type of concession	*FREEWAY*
Client	*Spanish Central Government*
Term	*20 Years (construction started in 2005 and operations began in 2007)*
Shareholder structure	
Shareholder	**Stake%**
Infraestructuras del futuro	*40%*
Coinfrasa	*25%*
Infravest	*35%*
Basic technical characteristics: 23 km freeway	
Basic construction details	
Builder	*Ute infraestructuras del futuro 30% + coinfrasa 70%*
Investment in civil engineering tendered	€51,568,352

Table 6.4 Total initial investment

Civil engineering	**Total investment**	**Depreciation period (for tax purposes) in years**
Earth moving, demolition, etc.	17,825,236	50
Infrastructures	26,252,632	50
Signage, etc.	3,693,558	18
Replacement of services	2,187,517	25
Miscellaneous, provisional deviations, health and safety	1,609,409	20
Total civil engineering	51,568,352	
Installations for traffic control	1, 804,260	18
Control and vigilance	1,122,000	35
Capitalized initial expenses	1,260,528	20
Expropriations[a]	4,366,033	20
Total initial investment in construction	60,121,172	

Notes: all amounts exclusive of VAT.

[a] This amount was forecast to compensate the owners of properties expropriated for the construction of the freeway.

Source: A R.

Table 6.5 Information on the financial structure (In € millions)

Type of finance	*Project finance*	
Financial institution	*Bank invest sa*	
Structure	**Current**	**Percentage %**
Equity	*12.00*	*16%*
Subordinated debt	*15.00*	*20%*
Senior debt	*45.00*	*59%*
Vat credit[a]	*3.75*	*5%*
Total	*75.75*[b]	*100%*

Notes: [a] This amount is a short-term credit to finance the Value Added Tax (VAT) generated for the purchases associated with the investments.
[b] This 75.75 is the total financing needed. This amount would build up over the first years to finance the total investment (60), the VAT (3.75) and the setting up of the equity (12).

6.3.3 The initial business plan

Osvaldo Martinez took a very active role in the development of the initial business plan, which included an estimate of the operating and financial aspects associated with the plans to build and operate the freeway. Appendix 6.5 gives the forecast schedule of the investments and their corresponding depreciation charges.

The forecast operating data associated with these investments are summarized by the free cash flow figures over the envisaged time frames, as shown in Appendix 6.6.

The free cash flows (FCF) associated with the investments in 2026 derived from the liquidation of the project as detailed in Table 6.6.

Table 6.7 summarizes the information on the costs of financing associated with the project.

Appendix 6.7 gives the expected schedule over time.

Finally, Table 6.8 summarizes some points from Appendixes 6.5, 6.6 and 6.7 (figures in rounded billions of euros).

The main covenant in the contracts defining the terms and conditions under which the loans were given stipulated that the average debt service coverage ratio (DSCR) was to remain over 1.5, throughout the life of the project. As of the second year of operation (2008) the DSCR had to be over 1.[4] The DSCR is defined as the ratio between the free cash flow and the total debt servicing, including interest and related charges.

According to the initial business plan, the theoretical return on the project (the IRR the FCF) was 7.18%, and the return due to the shareholders (the IRR of the shareholders' FCF) was 8.09%.[5]

Table 6.6 Projected value of the liquidation of the project (Figures in euros)

Gross book value 2026	60,121,172
Accumulated depreciation 2026	33,915,750
Net book value 2026	26,205,422
Estimated Liquidation liquidation value	15,000,000
Extraordinary profits	−11,205,422
Taxes saved	3,921,898
FCF associated with liquidation	18,921,898

Source: AR.

Table 6.7 Amount and costs of the financing (Figures in euros)

Associated financing	
VAT credit	3,750,000
Cost	5%
Subordinate debt	15,000,000
Cost	10%
Senior debt	45,000,000
Cost	6%

Source: AR.

Table 6.8 Some economic features of the Autopistas Radiales business plan

Expected negative FCF in 2004–2006	€58.4 billion
Expected Pay pay Back back period	13 years
Expected negative FCF to shareholders (2004–2013)	€18.3 billion

In 2004 the risk-free interest rate in Spain was around 2.00%, and in 2009 the level was 3.00%. See also Appendix 6.4.

6.3.4 The situation in 2009

In late spring 2009, as CFO of Autopistas Radiales, Martinez was aware of the importance of winding up the initial financing of the investments under circumstances very different from those originally envisaged when construction of the freeway began.

As a result of the drop in operating income growing out of the global financial crisis that began in 2007, the project's viability was seriously threatened. Up until 2008 the actual figures for the project's development had been fairly similar to those envisaged in the initial business plan. Although there

Table 6.9 Revised business plan

Business plan with changes	2008	2009	2010	2011	2012
Reduction in revenues	12%	10%	6%	4%	2%

had been some deviations from the investment plan, overall it had been implemented as anticipated. The main problem began to emerge in 2008, with the 12% drop against the initially forecast revenue, and an outlook for the future that anticipated no recovery before 2013.

At the beginning of 2009 the initial business plan was modified by factoring in a fall in revenues in line with expectations, as Table 6.9 shows.

From 2013 until 2026 projected revenues were assumed to be the same as the initial business plan, and the originally agreed financing would be maintained. Thus the return would fall to 7.02% for the project and 7.62% for shareholders (see Appendix 6.8).

This decline in shareholder returns was a consequence of the new capital investments needed to ensure the project's viability, as summarized in the forecast FCF schedule for shareholders.

Martínez believed that the new situation was basically unsustainable. Now the project would need an additional €2 million, and the current shareholders refused to agree to all the refinancing costs of the project coming out of their pockets. On the other hand, the financial institutions wanted to renegotiate costs and deadlines, due to the project's increased risk.

Martínez believed that operational and financial improvements would be needed to keep the project viable while offering at least a minimal return.

6.3.5 A possible solution

Following a proposal Martínez made at a meeting held on 15 May 2009, the AR Board of Directors agreed to begin exploring a sale of the company. As CFO and a member of the Board of Directors, Martínez knew that the initial investors were interested in a reasonable exit for their investment in AR. The Board appointed him to analyse what would be a reasonable price to aim for in negotiating the sale of the company.

As the reasonableness of the price would depend on one's perspective (i.e. that of the seller or the buyer), Martínez decided to begin by establishing the minimum price at which the current shareholders would have to sell the company in late 2009 to achieve the return of 7.62% derived from the modified business plan.

As Appendix 6.9 shows, he calculated that this would mean valuing the company at almost €70 million, as its debt stood at €51 million (subordinated and senior debt in 2009).

From the buyer's perspective, whether this price was attractive would depend on the new business plan for the company, a plan which introduced a series of improvements to both operating and financial aspects.

After an in-depth analysis of the possibilities for creating value in the company, Martínez summarized this new plan as follows:

A) Operational aspects
   - Income would reflect the drop in revenue shown in Table 6.7.
   - A series of operational improvements would be made, leading to a 10% reduction in operating costs in 2010, 5% in 2011 and 2% between 2012 and the end of the project.
   - Tax rate would be 35%, when applicable.

B) Financial aspects
   - The debt would be renegotiated, establishing a 10-year schedule of repayments as of 2012, with two years' grace in 2010 and 2011.
   - The new debt would have better conditions in terms of costs and debt service due to some additional public guarantees that would be available to the owners. These public guarantees came from the Spanish government's Ministry of Industry and were offered because of the public service provided by the freeway. According to these guarantees, in the next five years the Ministry would subsidize AR (if necessary) in order to have a ratio of FCF/total debt service no lower than 1.
   - Interest on debt would be set at 6%.

As CFO of Autopistas Radiales, Osvaldo Martínez was aware of the difficulty of completing a sale in the prevailing economic climate in Spain (and the rest of the euro area) in late spring 2009. The key challenge would be to find a price that would be reasonable for both parties.

If a sale proved impossible, Martínez wondered what other options the company might have in order to survive the crisis:

> It's going to be difficult to find a solution that makes the present shareholders happy...They want to leave the company, but also to minimize losses or avoid them, if possible. Well, it certainly will be difficult, but, at the end of the day, this is what I'm supposed to be paid for!

6.3.6 Some comments on the proposal

The case of AR describes the progress of a project finance operation from its beginnings in 2004, and the situation of the project in 2009 in the face of a crisis and the subsequent failure to meet with the initially expected cash flows. The case offers an excellent opportunity to discuss what to do when a project finance fails, analysing the alternative ways for ensuring the project's viability and profitability.

More specifically, we can:

- Analyse the fundamental characteristics of project finance (PF) from a financial point of view.
- Develop a financial analysis of PF, discussing legal constraints.
- Analyse the changes in the required return on investment brought about by changes in the initial conditions.
- Discuss alternative ways of ensuring the project's viability and profitability in the context of a crisis situation.

Looking back at this project from 2004, with hindsight and 2009 perspective, the whole idea of the investment decision may have been considered unrealistic. But when the game is over, it's very easy to bet on the final score.

In 2004, when the project was initially set up, it was a typical project finance (PF) operation in a unique situation: a booming economy, with plenty of liquidity, and market interest rates negative in real terms (during 2002–2004 in Spain interest rates were 2–2.8% and the inflation rate was 3–3.6%).

One of the points of interest in this case is to analyse a standard PF operation but in a peculiar economic and financial situation: Spain in 2004.

At the same time, financial institutions were interested in operations based on concessions of public services because of the implicit guarantee of public (government) institutions, with theoretically low operational risks. Private shareholders were interested in participating in the project because they would receive returns from being suppliers to the building and operation of the project, as well from their subsequent equity returns.

The combination of a booming economy, an unsustainable situation of market interest rates, the fact that a lot of financial institutions were willing to invest because they had a lot of liquidity, and an underestimation of operational risks (drop of revenues and operational earnings) associated with the project led to a very optimistic initial business plan.

There was no plan B for a less optimistic future scenario.

In order to analyse the alternatives available in mid-2009 it is worth understanding the scale of the problem.

Assuming that the financial institutions do not withdraw their financing from the project, when the shareholders' FCFs deriving from the original business plan are compared with those from the revised business plan, we can estimate the new capital needs the shareholders have to face as a result of the crisis.

Table 6.10 shows the most general case where there is no restriction on the dividend for legal reasons.

As well as the need for additional capital of almost two million euros, the loss of liquidity brought about by the changes the financial institutions want to impose, both in terms of costs and deadlines, also needs to be added.

If we compare the cash flows, bearing in mind the legal restriction on the distribution of dividends, the 1.9 million euros turn into 2.2 million euros:

Years	2004	2005	2006	2007	2008	2009	2010–2011	2012
Accumulated new financial needs	0	0	0	0	–14,901	–172,431	–172,431	–2,171,431

In short, the current shareholders of Autopistas Radiales face a short-term liquidity problem of 1.2 million euros, and the banks want to renegotiate costs and repayment terms on the syndicated loan.

In this context, the viability of the project calls for a renegotiation of the loans with the banks, a capital injection, or a possible sale of the project.

Assuming the new operators can implement the new business plan detailed in the case, they will get an economic return of 6.78% (IRR of the expected FCF to shareholders).

Clearly, this profitability is insufficient given the associated risk. In 2009 the risk-free interest rate was 3.00%. Expected cost of equity (Ke) for the seller/buyer would be around 9%, assuming a market premium of 4.00% and a beta of 1.5.

For the new shareholders there is no possibility of additional profits arising from their involvement in the project as builders or suppliers of materials for the construction. And it is necessary to adjust this return to take into account the legal restrictions on the availability of the expected FCFs.

As a consequence, present shareholders must be aware that the only way to sell the project to a new group is by accepting a very low final return in order to exit.

Table 6.10 Accumulated new financial needs of the project in 2009

Years	**2004**	**2005**	**2006**	**2007**	**2008**	**2009**	**2010**	**2011**	**2012**	**2013**	**2014**
FCF to shar in it BP	−6,526,811	−5,473,190	6,608,697	−3,224,545	−2,773,872	−2,325,235	−1,848,904	−1,358,443	−867,524	−403,726	1,443,075
FCF to shar rev BP	−6,526,811	−5,473,190	6,608,697	−3,224,545	−3,399,053	−2,872,485	−2,194,748	−1,601,284	−995,118	−403,726	1,443,075
New financial needs	0	0	0	0	−625,181	−547,250	−345,844	−242,841	−127,594	0	0
Accum new fin needs					−625,181	−1,172,431	−1,518,275	−1,761,116	−1,888,710	−1,888,710	−1,888,710

Table 6.11 Relationship between price of sale and economic return for seller and buyer

E(Equity Value)	Seller's return	Buyer's return	E/EBITDA
18,789,460	7.62%	6.78%	483
15,700,000	1.77%	7.91%	404
8,100,000	negative	12.04%	208
14,900,000	0.03%	8.23%	383

Table 6.11 shows a sensitivity analysis of the economic value of the Equity (E) in the eventual sale of AR and the associated economic return for the buyer and the seller in the operation. As we can see, if the seller wanted to keep the return of 7.62%, the price of the E should be €18.78 million and the expected return to the buyer only 6.78%. In order to get a reasonable minimum return to the buyer (12%), the Equity should be traded at €8.1 million, with a negative profitability for the sellers.

Another possible factor in the negotiation of the price may be the goodwill recognized in the transaction. The book value of E at the end of 2009 is around €9.3 million. To the extent that the buyer accepts a price above this amount it would be recognizing an economic value that exceeds the book value.

The question is, what negotiating power do the sellers (the current shareholders) have in this possible transaction?

It's clear that the negotiating power is in the hands of the potential buyers (the new shareholders), since they are the only ones able (eventually) to implement the new plan for the company. Sellers would probably have to make a fire sale (around a multiple of 2.5 for E/EBITDA, at the estimated accounting value of the Equity), given the legal situation of distress explained later.

Mr Martínez should present this situation very clearly to the present shareholders: an eventual sale of the company at the accounting value of the E in 2009 would be a very good exit for them. Most probably, buyers will offer a lower price than that.

At this point, Mr Martínez should also consider whether the present shareholders have alternatives to the eventual sale of AR. Of course, these alternatives will depend on the present situation of AR and the expected future of the company.

In 2009, the situation of AR is clear: the company is in a situation of distress, with a negative accounting value for the E. In the event of no sale, the only alternative to avoid legal liquidation is to increase capital by €11 million. Financial entities will only support the company if they believe the company will have more value after its restructuring than if it were liquidated now. Since the present owners are not able to set up a restructuring process, liquidation seems to be their only alternative.

Or, if possible, ask the government for financial help, given the public nature of the service AR is providing.

What actually happened?

After long negotiations with the eventual buyers, Mr Martínez and the selling group were unable to reach an agreement with the buyers on the price for AR. With public support from the Spanish government in the form of guarantees, AR was able to restructure the operation late in 2009 and to get a bridge loan of €10 million, in order to avoid liquidation.

As the economic situation in Spain in 2010–2012 became very negative and after receiving additional subventions from the Spanish government, at the beginning of 2013 the AR company may turn out to be the first PF ever to be bailed out by the Spanish government.

Appendices

Appendix 6.1 Accounting information on Famosa (Millions of euros)

	2008	2009
Revenues	167.4	162.3
Trade discounts	–22.1	–24.3
Net sales	145.3	137.9
Cost of sales	–61.2	–60.2
Gross margin	84.1	77.8
Other revenues	0.8	0.0
Capitalized expenses	9.2	5.7
Variable operating expenses:	–25.6	–27.7
Royalties	–6.1	–7.0
Commissions	–0.9	–1.0
Marketing and development	–11.1	–12.4
Transport	–7.5	–7.4
Variable margin	68.5	55.7
Fixed operating expenses:	–46.3	–41.2
Personnel	–29.1	–25.1
R and D	–0.5	0.0
Leases	–4.0	–4.9
Repair and maintenance	–2.1	–0.3
General services	–1.3	–2.4
Materials	–3.9	–3.1
Other services	–4.1	–4.0
Other fixed expenses	–1.3	–1.4
EBITDA	22.2	14.6
Depreciation and amortization expenses	–19.8	–13.6
EBIT	2.4	1.0

Appendix 6.2 Summary of estimated operating results for Famosa (Millions of euros)

Years	2010	2011	2012	2013	2014	2015	2016
Revenues	164.0	173.3	186.7	190.4	196.2	202.0	208.1
Trade discounts	–22.3	–22.3	–24.0	–24.5	–25.2	–26.0	–26.8
Net sales	141.6	151.0	162.7	165.9	170.9	176.1	181.3
Cost of sales	–57.6	–64.1	–73.0	–74.4	–76.6	–78.9	–81.3
Gross margin	84.0	86.9	89.7	91.5	94.3	97.1	100.0
Other revenues	0.2	0.2	0.2	0.2	0.2	0.2	0.2
Capitalized expenses	5.2	5.2	5.3	5.3	5.3	5.3	5.0
Variable operating expenses:	–27.8	–28.2	–29.6	–30.0	–30.6	–31.3	–32.0
Royalties	–7.2	–6.3	–6.5	–6.5	–6.5	–6.5	–6.5
Commissions	–1.2	–1.4	–1.6	–1.6	–1.6	–1.6	–1.6
Marketing and development	–12.7	–13.4	–13.7	–14.0	–14.4	–14.9	–15.3
Transport	–6.6	–7.1	–7.7	–7.9	–8.1	–8.3	–8.6
Variable margin	61.6	64.1	65.6	67.0	69.1	71.3	73.2
Fixed operating expenses:	–42.9	–42.8	–42.7	–43.1	–43.6	–44.0	–44.5
Personnel	–26.4	–25.5	–25.7	–25.9	–26.2	–26.5	–26.8
R and D	0.0	0.0	0.0	0.0	0.0	0.0	0.0
Leases	–4.8	–5.0	–3.7	–3.8	–3.8	–3.9	–3.9
Repair and maintenance	–0.3	–0.3	–0.3	–0.3	–0.3	–0.3	–0.3
General services	–2.8	–3.3	–3.9	–4.0	–4.0	–4.1	–4.1
Materials	–3.2	–3.1	–3.3	–3.3	–3.3	–3.4	–3.4
Other services	–3.9	–4.0	–4.1	–4.1	–4.2	–4.2	–4.3
Other fixed expenses	–1.6	–1.6	–1.6	–1.6	–1.6	–1.7	–1.7
EBITDA	18.6	21.2	23.0	23.9	25.5	27.2	28.8
Depreciation and amortization expenses	–14.4	–14.4	–14.4	–5.1	–5.6	–6.2	–6.7
EBIT	4.3	6.9	8.6	18.8	20.0	21.1	22.1

Appendix 6.3 Famosa: Estimated cash flows associated to the business plan (Figures in millions euros)

Years	2010	2011	2012	2013	2014	2015	2016
EBIT	4.3	6.9	8. 6	18.8	20.0	21.1	22.1
Taxes on EBIT	0.0	0.0	0.0	–2.7	–6.0	–6.3	–6.6
EBIaT	4.3	6.9	8.6	16.0	14.0	14.7	15.4
Deprec & Amort	14.4	14.4	14.4	5.1	5.6	6.2	6.7
Operational FCC	18.6	21.2	23.0	21.2	19.6	20.9	22.1
FCF fron WC variation	–0.1	–0.4	–0.5	–0.2	–0.3	–0.4	–0.4
FCF fron Capex	–5.7	–5.3	–5.1	–5.1	–5.2	–5.3	–5.0
Total FCF	12.8	15.5	17.3	15.8	14.0	15.3	16.8

In order to predict the likelihood of producing enough free cash flow to cover the payment of debt interest, we must use the information available to estimate the debt capacity of the company for servicing between 2010 and 2016.

Assuming that all free cash flow is dedicated to cover the service of debt, and that the super-senior debt is amortized before the syndicated loan, we obtain the following:

Estimated debt repayment: Figures in millions euros

Years	2010	2011	2012	2013	2014	2015	2016
Syndicated Debt							
Initial Debt	77.7	77.7	77.7	75.4	68.6	61.9	53.5
Amortization of principal	0.0	0.0	–2.3	–6.8	–6.7	–8.4	–10.6
Final Debt	77.7	77.7	75.4	68.6	61.9	53.5	43.0
Financial Expenses	–5.1	–5.1	–5.1	–4.9	–4.5	–4.0	–3.5
New lines of credit (super- senior)							
Initial Debt	11.1	9.2	4.5	0.0	0.0	0.0	0.0
Amortization of principal	–1.9	–4.7	–4.5	0.0	0.0	0.0	0.0
Final Debt	9.2	4.5	0.0	0.0	0.0	0.0	0.0
Financial Expenses	–0.7	–0.6	–0.3	0.0	0.0	0.0	0.0
Total Cash Financial Expenses	–5.8	–5.6	–5.3	–4.9	–4.5	–4.0	–3.5
Capitalized syndicate loan							
Initial Debt Capitalized	32.5	35.1	37.9	40.9	44.2	47.8	51.6
Amortization of principal	0.0	0.0	0.0	0.0	0.0	0.0	0.0
Final Debt Capitalized	35.1	37.9	40.9	44.2	47.8	51.6	55.7
Financial Expenses Capitalized	–2.6	–2.8	–3.0	–3.3	–3.5	–3.8	–4.1
Total Financial Expenses	–8.4	–8.5	–8.4	–8.2	–8.0	–7.8	–7.6

Based on this estimated figures we can forecast the expected Free Cash Flow for Shareholders:

Years	2010	2011	2012	2013	2014	2015	2016
Figures in millions euros							
Total FCF	12.8	15.5	17.3	15.8	14.0	15.3	16.8
Financial Expenses × (1–t)	–8.4	–8.5	–8.4	–7.0	–5.6	–5.5	–5.3
Capitalized Financial Exp	2.6	2.8	3.0	3.3	3.5	3.8	4.1
Capitalized Expenses	–5.2	–5.2	–5.3	–5.3	–5.3	–5.3	–5.0
To Amortization of principal	1.9	4.7	6.7	6.8	6.7	8.4	10.6
FCF for Shareholders	0.0	0.0	0.0	0.0	0.0	0.0	0.0

Appendix 6.4 Historical economic information about Spain (Figures in Percentages)

Year	GDP Growth Rate	Unemployment Rate	Inflation Rate	Interest Rate
2002	2.7%	11.3%	3.6%	2.75%
2003	3.0%	11.1%	3.1%	2.0%
2004	3.2%	10.6%	3.1%	2.0%
2005	3.5%	9.2%	3.4%	2.3%
2006	4.0%	9.8%	3.6%	3.5%
2007	3.6%	8.4%	2.8%	4.0%
2008	0.9%	11.4%	4.1%	2.5%
2009	–3.7%	18.0%	–0.2%	3.0%

Source: http://www.bde.es/f/webbde/SES/Secciones/Publicaciones/InformesBoletinesRevistas/BoletinEconomico/06/Dic/Fich/indica.pdf.

Appendix 6.5 Forecast Schedule of investments and depreciation for Autopistas Radiales (Figures in euros)

Exhibit 2

Years	**2004**	**2005**	**2006**	**2007**	**2008**	**2009**	**2010**	**2011**	**2012**	**2013**	**2014**
Capex Evolution											
Capitalized initial expenses	1,260,528										
Expropriations	4,366,033										
Earth moving, demolition, etc.		17,825,236									
Infrastructures		26,252,632									
Signage, etc.			3,693,558								
Replacement of services			2,187,517								
Misc. provl. dev. health and safety			1,609,409								
Installations to traffic control				1,804,260							
Control and vigilance				1,122,000							
Total Capex excluding VAT	5,626,561	44,077,868	7,490,484	2,926,260	0	0	0	0	0	0	0
Supported VAT	900,250	7,052,459	1,198,477								
Recovering of VAT		–900,250	–7,052,459	–1,198,477							
Total Capex including VAT	6,526,811	50,230,077	1,636,502	1,727,783	0	0	0	0	0	0	0
Expected depreciation											
Depreciation for init. exp. and expr.		1,125,312	1,125,312	1,125,312	1,125,312	1,125,312	0	0	0	0	0
Depreciation for earth mov. and infr.			881,557	881,557	881,557	881,557	881,557	881,557	881,557	881,557	881,557
Depreciation for signature and repl. serv.				453,639	453,639	453,639	453,639	453,639	453,639	453,639	453,639
Depreciation for installation and control					132,294	132,294	132,294	132,294	132,294	132,294	132,294
Total Depreciation Expenses		1,125,132	2,006,870	2,460,509	2,592,803	2,592,803	1,467,490	1,467,490	1,467,490	1,467,490	1,467,490

Years	2015	2016	2017	2018	2019	2020	2021	2022	2023	2024	2025
Capex Evolution											
Capitalized initial expenses											
Expropriations											
Earth moving, demolition, etc.											
Infrastructures											
Signage, etc.											
Replacement of services											
Misc. provl. dev. health and safety											
Installations to traffic control											
Control and vigilance											
Total Capex excluding VAT	0	0	0	0	0	0	0	0	0	0	0
Supported VAT											
Recovering of VAT											
Total Capex including VAT	0	0	0	0	0	0	0	0	0	0	0
Expected depreciation											
Depreciation for init. exp. and expr	0	0	0	0	0	0	0	0	0	0	0
Depreciation for earth mov. and infr.	881,557	881,557	881,557	881,557	881,557	881,557	881,557	881,557	881,557	881,557	881,557
Depreciation for signature and repl. serv.	453,639	453,639	453,639	453,639	453,639	453,639	453,639	453,639	453,639	453,639	453,639
Depreciation for installation and control	132,294	132,294	132,294	132,294	132,294	132,294	132,294	132,294	132,294	132,294	132,294
Total Depreciation Expenses	1,467,490	1,467,490	1,467,490	1,467,490	1,467,490	1,467,490	1,467,490	1,467,490	1,467,490	1,467,490	1,467,490

Source: Initial Business Plan (estimates).

Appendix 6.6 AR: Expected schedule of the FCF associated with the project (Figures in euros)

Years	2004	2005	2006	2007	2008	2009	2010	2011	2012	2013	2014
Revenues				2,479,476	5,209,838	5,472,505	5,764,072	6,071,018	6,379,719	6,662,641	8,329,954
Personal expenses				310,483	612,671	635,952	660,118	685,203	711,241	738,268	766,322
External services and other expenses				20,384	39,913	41,110	42,344	43,614	44,922	46,270	47,658
Maintenance expenses				162,572	318,327	327,877	337,713	347,845	358,280	389,029	380,099
Total operational expenses (excluding Taxes)				493,439	970,911	1,004,940	1,040,175	1,076,662	1,114,443	1,153,566	1,194,079
Taxes on operations (IAE)				32,800	32,800	32,800	32,800	32,800	32,800	32,800	32,800
Total operational expenses				526,239	1,003,711	1,037,740	1,072,975	1,109,462	1,147,243	1,186,366	1,226,879
EBITDA				1,953,237	4,206,128	4,434,765	4,691,096	4,961,557	5,232,476	5,476,274	7,103,075
Depreciation expenses		−1,125,312	−2,006,870	−2,460,509	−2,592,803	−2,592,803	−1,467,490	−1,467,490	−1,467,490	−1,467,490	−1,467,490
EBIT		−1,125,312	−2,006,870	−507,271	1,613,325	1,841,962	3,223,606	3,494,066	3,764,985	4,008,784	5,635,584
Taxes		0	0	0	0	0	0	0	0	0	0
EBIaT		−1,125,312	−2,006,870	−507,271	1,613,325	1,841,962	3,223,606	3,494,066	3,764,985	4,008,784	5,635,584
Depreciation		1,125,312	2,006,870	2,480,509	2,592,803	2,592,803	1,467,490	1,467,490	1,467,490	1,467,490	1,467,490
FCF from operations		0	0	1,953,237	4,206,128	4,434,765	4,691,096	4,961,557	5,232,476	5,476,274	7,103,075
FCF from Capex	−6,526,811	−50,230,077	−1,636,502	−1,727,783	0	0	0	0	0	0	0
Total FCF	−6,526,811	−50,230,077	−1,636,502	225,455	4,206,128	4,434,765	4,691,098	4,981,557	5,232,476	5,476,274	7,103,075

Years	2015	2016	2017	2018	2019	2020	2021	2022	2023	2024	2025	2026
Revenues	8,721,594	9,155,216	9,562,081	10,012,463	10,484,230	11,006,218	11,495,995	12,038,064	12,606,717	13,235,917	13,749,684	14,162,175
Personal expenses	795,442	825,669	857,044	889,612	923,417	958,507	994,930	1,032,738	1,071,982	1,112,717	1,155,000	1,198,890
External services and other expenses	49,088	50,560	52,077	53,640	55,249	56,906	58,613	60,372	62,183	64,048	65,970	67,949
Maintenance expenses	391,502	403,248	415,345	427,805	440,639	453,859	467,474	481,499	495,944	510,822	526,147	541,931
Total operational expenses (excluding Taxes)	1,236,032	1,279,477	1,324,466	1,371,057	1,419,305	1,469,272	1,521,018	1,574,608	1,630,108	1,687,587	1,747,117	1,808,770
Taxes on operations (IAE)	32,800	32,800	32,800	32,800	32,800	32,800	32,800	32,800	32,800	32,800	32,800	32,800
Total operational expenses	1,268,832	1,312,277	1,357,266	1,403,857	1,452,105	1,502,072	1,553,818	1,607,408	1,662,908	1,720,387	1,779,917	1,841,570
EBITDA	7,452,762	7,842,939	8,204,815	8,608,606	9,032,124	9,504,146	9,942,177	10,430,656	10,943,808	11,515,530	11,969,767	12,320,604
Depreciation expenses	–1,467,490	–1,467,490	–1,306,549	–1,306,549	–1,306,549	–1,306,549	–1,306,549	–1,306,549	–1,306,549	–1,306,549	–1,206,313	–1,206,313
EBIT	5,985,271	6,375,449	6,898,265	7,302,057	7,725,575	8,197,597	8,635,628	9,124,107	9,637,259	10,208,980	10,763,455	11,114,292
Taxes	0	0	–193,818	–2,555,720	–2,703,951	–2,869,159	–3,022,470	–3,193,437	–3,373,041	–3,573,143	–3,767,209	–3,890,002
EBIaT	5,985,271	6,375,449	5,984,447	4,746,337	5,021,624	5,328,438	5,613,158	5,930,669	6,264,218	6,635,837	6,996,245	7,224,290
Depreciation	1,467,490	1,467,490	1,306,549	1,306,549	1,306,549	1,306,549	1,306,549	1,306,549	1,306,549	1,306,549	1,206,313	1,206,313
FCF from operations	7,452,762	7,842,939	7,290,997	6,052,886	6,328,173	6,634,987	6,919,708	7,237,219	7,570,768	7,942,387	8,202,558	8,430,602
FCF from Capex	0	0	0	0	0	0	0	0	0	0	0	18,921,898
Total FCF	7,452,762	7,842,939	7,290,997	6,052,886	6,328,173	6,634,987	6,919,708	7,237,219	7,570,768	7,942,387	8,202,558	27,352,500

Source: Initial Business Plan (estimates).

Appendix 6.7 AR: Forecast schedule of debt servicing (Figures in euros)

Years	2004	2005	2006	2007	2008	2009	2010	2011	2012	2013	2014
Total FCF	−6,526,811	−50,230,077	−1,636,502	225,455	4,206,128	4,434,765	4,691,096	4,961,557	5,232,476	5,476,274	7,103,075
VAT Credit	0	3,750,000	−3,750,000								
Financial Expenses (1–t)		0	−187,500								
Subordinated Debt	0	15,000,000	15,000,000	14,000,000	13,000,000	12,000,000	11,000,000	10,000,000	9,000,000	8,000,000	7,000,000
Financial Expenses (1–t)			−1,500,000	−1,500,000	−1,400,000	−1,300,000	−1,200,000	−1,100,000	−1,000,000	−900,000	−800,000
Senior Debt		26,006,887	45,000,000	43,000,000	41,000,000	39,000,000	37,000,000	35,000,000	33,000,000	31,000,000	29,000,000
Financial Expenses (1–t)			−1,560,413	−2,700,000	−2,580,000	−2,460,000	−2,340,000	−2,220,000	−2,100,000	−1,980,000	−1,860,000
New Credits/ Repayments	0	44,756,887	11,493,113	750,000	−3,000,000	−3,000,000	−3,000,000	−3,000,000	−3,000,000	−3,000,000	−3,000,000
FCF for Shareholders	−6,526,811	−5,473,190	6,608,697	−3,224,545	−2,773,872	−2,325,235	−1,848,904	−1,358,443	−867,524	−403,726	1,443,075

Years	2015	2016	2017	2018	2019	2020	2021	2022	2023	2024	2025	2026
Total FCF	7,452,762	7,842,939	7,290,997	6,052,886	6,328,173	6,634,987	6,919,708	7,237,219	7,570,768	7,942,387	8,202,558	27,352,500
VAT Credit												
Financial Expenses(1–t)												
Subordinated Debt	6,000,000	5,000,000	4,000,000	3,000,000	2,000,000	1,000,000	0	0	0	0	0	0
Financial Expenses(1–t)	–700,000	–600,000	–433,765	–260,000	–195,000	–130,000	–65,000	0	0	0	0	0
Senior Debt	27,000,000	25,000,000	23,000,000	21,000,000	19,000,000	17,000,000	15,000,000	13,000,000	11,000,000	9,000,000	7,000,000	0
Financial Expenses(1–t)	–1,740,000	–1,620,000	–1,301,294	–897,000	–819,000	–741,000	–663,000	–585,000	–507,000	–429,000	–351,000	–273,000
New Credits/ Repayments	–3,000,000	–3,000,000	–3,000,000	–3,000,000	–3,000,000	–3,000,000	–3,000,000	–2,000,000	–2,000,000	–2,000,000	–2,000,000	–7,000,000
FCF for Shareholders	2,012,762	2,622,939	2,555,938	1,895,886	2,314,173	2,763,987	3,191,708	4,652,219	5,063,768	5,513,387	5,851,558	20,079,500

Note: As stated in the case, as of 2008, and in the years in which the forecast FCF for shareholders is negative, shareholders will need to pay in to a reserve fund.

Source: Initial Business Plan (estimates).

Appendix 6.8 Expected schedule of the project's FCF and FCF to shareholders in the revised business plan (Figures in euros)

Years	2004	2005	2006	2007	2008	2009	2010	2011	2012	2013	2014
Total FCF	−6,526,811	−50,230,077	−1,636,502	225,455	4,206,128	4,434,765	4,691,096	4,961,557	5,232,476	5,476,274	7,103,075
VAT Credit	0	3,750,000	−3,750,000								
Financial Expenses (1−t)		0	−187,500								
Subordinated Debt	0	15,000,000	15,000,000	14,000,000	13,000,000	12,000,000	11,000,000	10,000,000	9,000,000	8,000,000	7,000,000
Financial Expenses (1−t)		0	−1,500,000	−1,500,000	−1,400,000	−1,300,000	−1,200,000	−1,100,000	−1,000,000	−900,000	−800,000
Senior Debt		26,006,887	45,000,000	43,000,000	41,000,000	39,000,000	37,000,000	35,000,000	33,000,000	31,000,000	29,000,000
Financial Expenses (1−t)			−1,560,413	−2,700,000	−2,580,000	−2,460,000	−2,340,000	−2,220,000	−2,100,000	−1,980,000	−1,860,000
New Credits/ Repayments	0	44,756,887	11,493,113	750,000	−3,000,000	−3,000,000	−3,000,000	−3,000,000	−3,000,000	−3,000,000	−3,000,000
FCF for Shareholders	−6,526,811	−5,473,190	6,608,697	−3,224,545	−2,773,872	−2,325,235	−1,848,904	−1,358,443	−867,524	−403,726	1,443,075

Years	2015	2016	2017	2018	2019	2020	2021	2022	2023	2024	2025	2026
Total FCF	7,452,762	7,842,939	7,290,997	6,052,886	6,328,173	6,634,987	6,919,708	7,237,219	7,570,768	7,942,387	8,202,558	27,352,500
VAT Credit												
Financial Expenses(1–t)												
Subordinated Debt	6,000,000	5,000,000	4,000,000	3,000,000	2,000,000	1,000,000	0	0	0	0	0	0
Financial Expenses(1–t)	–700,000	–600,000	–433,765	–260,000	–195,000	–130,000	–65,000	0	0	0	0	0
Senior Debt	27,000,000	25,000,000	23,000,000	21,000,000	19,000,000	17,000,000	15,000,000	13,000,000	11,000,000	9,000,000	7,000,000	0
Financial Expenses(1–t)	–1,740,000	–1,620,000	–1,301,294	–897,000	–819,000	–741,000	–663,000	–585,000	–507,000	–429,000	–351,000	–273,000
New Credits/ Repayments	–3,000,000	–3,000,000	–3,000,000	–3,000,000	–3,000,000	–3,000,000	–3,000,000	–2,000,000	–2,000,000	–2,000,000	–2,000,000	–7,000,000
FCF for Shareholders	2,012,762	2,622,939	2,555,938	1,895,886	2,314,173	2,763,987	3,191,708	4,652,219	5,063,768	5,513,387	5,851,558	20,079,500

Notes: RR of FCF for the project = 7.02%
IRR of FCF to Shareholders = 7.62%

Appendix 6.9 Estimated price of the equity in 2009 to achieve a shareholders' return similar to the one in the revised business plan (Figures in euros)

Years	**2004**	**2005**	**2006**	**2007**	**2008**	**2009**
FCF to shareholders	−6,526,811	−5,473,190	6,608,697	−3,224,545	−3,399,053	−2,872,485
TV at 2009						18,789,460
Total FCF to shareholders	−6,526,811	−5,473,190	6,608,697	−3,224,545	−3,399,053	15,916,975
IRR	7.62%					
Debt	51,000,000					
Equity	18,789,460					
EV	69,789,460					

Note: Column 6 shows the theoretical price for which the initial shareholders should sell the company at the end of 2009 to get an economic return of 7.62%, which is the modified profitability associated with the revision of the initial business plan, including the drop in revenues of 12% and 10% in 2008 and 2009.

7
Some Examples of Restructuring (II)

7.1 Introduction

In this chapter we continue our review of some real examples of restructuring's processes in different companies, operating in different industries and dealing with different circumstances. In our analysis we will try to clarify why these companies were running short of cash and what actions were implemented in order to fix the situation.

7.2 Preparing a sale: the acquisition of Foster's by SABMiller

On 21 September 2011, SABMiller plc ('SABMiller') announced that it had agreed with Foster's Group Limited ('Foster's') on a recommended cash offer to Foster's shareholders at A$5.40 per share, which values Foster's equity at approximately A$9.9 billion (€8 billion).

Previously, on 21 June 2011, SABMiller had made an offer at A$ 4.9 per share, but this offer was rejected by Foster's Board of Directors. By acquiring Foster now at a price of A$5.40 per share, SABMiller was paying a goodwill of A$9.5 billion, for a company that in the last two years had negative profit after taxes attributable to its shareholders (–464.4 and –89.0, in 2010 and 2011, respectively).[1]

In 2011 the Revenues of Foster's were A$2.56 billion, and its Equity at accounting value was A$0.4 billion. It's obvious that paying A$9.9 for the Equity only made sense if we consider that Foster's would generate economic value in the SABMiller Group.

7.2.1 Some information on the industry

Global beer consumption volumes was over 1.91 billion hectolitres in the year ended 31 December 2010, with the global economic downturn exacerbating volume declines in some countries, particularly in Europe and in the United States. The global beer market had been growing at an average rate of 2.9% per annum over the five years ended in 31 December 2010, and forecast an average growth rate of 2.7% between 2011 and 2016.

The emerging markets such as Africa, Latin America, China and India account for the bulk of the growth in global beer consumption. By contrast, the mature markets of North America, Western Europe and Australasia have generated relatively flat sales volumes in recent years. Beer consumption on a per capita basis in the United States, United Kingdom, Canada and Australia has been in decline for a prolonged period. Developed beer market volumes are expected to remain flat or marginally decline.

According to the Canadian Global Beer Trends Report, that summarizes the top 20 global beer markets by volume in the 2010 calendar year and the forecasted compound annual growth rate by region for the period 2011 to 2016, China is currently the largest beer market in the world by volume and also one of the fastest growing ones, characterized in recent years by rapidly increasing production, market consolidation and improved efficiency. Continued strong volume growth is expected as per capita consumption increases. Price increases are expected to improve profitability, after having remained largely unchanged for an extended period of time.

India is expected to continue to grow volumes at double digit rates, with significant population and consumption upside (current per capita consumption is less than two litres per year). However, factors such as a restrictive regulatory environment, limited affordability and infrastructure limitations associated with a large percentage of the population residing in rural areas, as well as cultural influences affecting alcohol consumption, may present some impediments in this market. Strong volume growth in Africa and Latin America is expected to result from the younger demographics and affluence resulting in increased incomes.

7.2.2 Some information on the companies

SABMiller is one of the world's largest brewers, with brewing interests and distribution agreements across six continents. SABMiller's portfolio includes global brands such as Pilsner Urquell, Peroni Nastro Azzurro, Miller Genuine Draft and Grolsch. SABMiller is also one of the world's largest bottlers of Coca-Cola products. Headquartered in London, United Kingdom, SABMiller has its primary listing on the London Stock Exchange and its secondary listing on the Johannesburg Stock Exchange.

Foster's is an Australian-based producer and marketer of beer and cider. The portfolio of brands produced by, or licensed to, Foster's includes the leaders in the traditional regular, premium domestic and premium international beer segments and the leading cider brand in Australia. Some of Foster's brands are also sold internationally.

Foster's was primarily focused on brewing activities with the majority of its sales revenue and earnings generated by its Australian and Pacific beer business, Carlton United Brewers, (approximately 98% of its net sales revenues and EBIT in the 2011 financial year) and the remainder by the rest of world business. The rest of world business generated earnings from the sales, licensing and distribution of its Australian beer brands in markets outside Australia and the Pacific and from a distribution joint-venture in the Middle East.

Carlton United Brewers experienced a decline in market share – based on packaged (off-premise) beer volumes – from 55.0% in the 2001 financial year to 49.3% in the 2011 financial year. This share loss was primarily attributable to Foster's beer portfolio being weighted heavily towards lower-growth segments (e.g. traditional regular), notwithstanding that Foster's has stated that it is undertaking initiatives to rebalance its portfolio.

7.2.3 Foster's actions

In 2006, Foster's began to divest non-core businesses and assets in line with the company's announced strategy to focus on premium beverages. Foster's sold the 'Foster's' brand in Europe to its brewing and distribution partner, Scottish & Newcastle plc ('Scottish & Newcastle'), for $750 million. In addition, Foster's exited its brewing operations in the Asian region, with the sale of its Chinese, Vietnamese and Indian breweries.

Foster's announced a restructuring initiative focused on a multi-beverage strategy whereby Foster's sales force, supply chain, marketing and consumer insights teams, as well as infrastructure, were shared across all product categories, and three new regional businesses were created. However, unsatisfactory performance of the wine business following the restructure led to a detailed review of the company's wine business in 2008. The review resulted in the disbandment of the multi-beverage model and the structural separation of the Australian beer and wine businesses.

In May 2010, Foster's announced its intention to create separate ASX-listed companies for the beer and the wine businesses via a demerger. As a consequence of this divesting process, the balance sheet of Foster's changed dramatically, as shown in Table 7.1.

7.2.4 The announcement

On 21 September 2011, Foster's Group Limited announced that it had entered into a Scheme Implementation Deed with SABMiller plc under

Table 7.1 Evolution of Foster's balance sheet (Figures in millions of A$)

Year	2010	2011
Cash	236.7	58.3
Receivables	990.3	542.7
Inventories	1,012.8	157.8
Other assets	45.7	0.0
Total Current Assets	2,285.5	758.8
Net Material Fixed Assets	2,315.8	769.1
Net Immaterial FA	1,898.5	910.9
Deferred tax assets	330.0	558.5
Total Assets	6,829.8	2,997.3
Payables	806.4	498.0
Other current liabilities	188.3	141.3
Deferred tax liabilities	555.2	282.6
Debt	2,564.5	1,675.8
Equity	2,715.4	399.6
Total L+E	6,829.8	2,997.3

which SABMiller acquired all the shares in Foster's. Foster's shareholders received a total of $5.40 cash per share.

The proposal consideration fairly reflects the strategic attractiveness of Foster, its leading market position in the Australian beer industry and the potential to improve Foster's financial and operating performance. Whilst Foster's management is forecasting considerable earnings growth over the next five years, this growth is subject to a range of uncertainties and risks, many of which are outside of the control of Foster's. In the short term, an improvement in earnings is dependent on a recovery in economic conditions and consumer confidence resulting in a revival of the beer market.

The valuation of Foster's is the aggregate of the estimated market value of its operating business and non-trading assets less external borrowings and non-trading liabilities as at 30 June 2011.

As a result of the combination of both companies, total revenues have shown constant growth (see Table 7.2).

7.2.5 Some comments on the operation

As mentioned earlier, Foster's price offered by SABMiller only makes sense in the context of a strategic acquisition on the grounds of a company already restructured.

Evaluating Foster's in a continuity scenario, both in terms of FCF and Terminal Value,[2] the expected economic profitability of the operation

Table 7.2 Five-year financial review

Five-year financial review for the years ended 31 March					
	2013	2012	2011	2010	2009
Group revenue (US$m)	34,487	31,388	28,311	26,350	25,302
EBITA (US$m)	6,421	5,634	5,044	4,381	4,129
EBITA margin (%)	18.6	17.9	17.8	16.6	16.3
Adjusted EPS (US cents)	238.7	214.8	191.5	161.1	137.5
Dividends per share (US cents)	101.0	91.0	81.0	68.0	58.0
Sales volumes (million hl)					
Lager	242	229	218	213	210
Soft drinks	57	49	46	44	44

Source: SABMiller Annual Reports.

Table 7.3 A summary of some key points

Deal: A$ 9,900 million in cash for E of Foster	
Key point: conservative valuation + price in 5 year equal to present price (14.3 times EBITDA for EV)	
Economic profitability of the operation (on Assets)	9.15%
Economic profitability for shareholders:	
All FCF to service of debt	12.77%
All FCF to service of debt (2012–2014)	
Last two years, keep the capital structure constant, in percentage terms.	
Apparent profitability	15.63%
ROA	6.92%
ROE	8.39%

would be 9.2%. The economic profitability for the shareholders would depend on how the acquisition is financed.

In an evaluation scenario, assuming a five-year horizon and a financing of A$9.9 billion, 56% in Equity and 44% Debt, and further assuming that all the FCF generated in the five years is used to cover the service of the debt, the economic profitability for the new shareholders would be 12.8%.

In the same scenario, if we assume that in the first three years all the FCF are dedicated to cover the service of the debt, and in the last two years we keep a constant capital structure (63% E and 37% D), then the economic profitability for the new shareholders would be 15.6%. Table 7.3 summarizes some key information on this acquisition.

Appendix 7.2 also shows additional information on this acquisition.

7.3 Restructuring to grow: the cases of eDream and OdigeO

A good thing about a crisis is that it helps to clean up inefficiencies. This is particularly true in some activities, like in the private equity industry. A period of crisis like the one that began in 2007 is helping a lot of firms to realize the importance of having an appropriate methodology to analyse targets.

Let's consider the case of Permira and the strategy developed in the acquisition and development of eDream, in 2010.

As an investing fund, Permira was looking for investments in industries with potential growth, good profitability and trending to future concentration. The company had two secondary criteria: avoid overpricing and a clear exit strategy in a reasonable period of time (around 5 years).

Applying these ideas and criteria, in 2009 Permira identified an interesting industry to invest in: Online Travel Agencies (OTAs). After a careful research of the leading companies operating in that sector, Permira decided to buy eDreams, a leading OTA in Europe.

7.3.1 Why eDreams?

They selected eDreams because:

1) It was one of the Europe's top independent OTAs.
2) It had a leading position in high growth markets.
3) It had a superior business model:
   - unique alignment with consumers;
   - no inventory risk, strong cash generation;
   - highly scalable for growth; and
   - productive and resilient to downturn (low fixed costs).
4) It had a strong P and L and Balance Sheet.
5) It had a seasoned team with strong international and large corporate exposure.
6) The industry had strong and sustainable entry barriers in:
   - marketing mix;
   - leading technology platform;
   - customers and suppliers; and
   - economies of scale.

With a recurrent EBITDA of €21 million, eDreams also had room for improvements in control systems, accounting and cash management.

The final price for the Enterprise Value (EV) was €252 million, equivalent to a multiple of 12 times EBITDA.

Why this price? Because with a recurrent EBITDA of €21 million, eDreams had an estimated recurrent FCF of €14 million. Assuming a capital structure of 50% Debt, a cost of the debt of 6%, and an estimated cost of Equity around 12%, the EV of €252 million required a Terminal Value with a permanent growth around 2.46%. See more details in Tables 7.4 and 7.5.

7.3.2 Only eDreams?

In any case, the acquisition of eDreams was a first step towards building up a European-wide operation. Permira considered that the OTA industry will remain having a strong and sustainable growth, since the migration to online will continue in the coming years. Margins were expected to remain stable or to expand, and there were opportunities for growth based in M and A.

In June 2011 Permira set up a merger of three European companies operating in the OTA industry: eDreams, based in Barcelona; goVoyages, based in Paris; and OdigeO, based in London.

Table 7.4 Estimated permanent FCF of eDreams

Recurrent FCF	
EBITDA	21
DA	–2
EBIT	19
Taxes	–5
Change in WC	5
Capex	–5
FCF	14

Table 7.5 Valuation of eDreams

Cap Ex structure	
E	50.0%
D	50.0%
V	100.0%
Kd	6.0%
Ke	12.0%
t	25.0%
WACC	8.25%
g	2.46%
EV	252

The synergies in the M and A process were estimated at €20 million, as a result of:

- Centralized pricing, marketing and technologies.
- Sharing inventories, processes and technologies.
- Getting better prices from suppliers: insurance companies, airlines.
- Setting up a special agreement with Amadeus.

Additionally, creating a bigger company improved the opportunities for Permira to get a good exit after some years. More specifically, it could exit by setting up an IPO.

The new eDreams group was valued at an EV of €1,296 million, based on a multiple of 12 times EBITDA. Estimated FCF was €64 million, as detailed in Table 7.6.

Assuming a capital structure of 42% Debt, a cost of the debt of 6%, and an estimated cost of Equity around 12%, the EV of €1,296 million required a Terminal Value with a permanent growth around 3.77% (Table 7.7).

Table 7.6 Estimated FCF for the new eDreams group (Figures in millions of euros)

EBITDA	108
DA	−6
EBIT	102
Taxes	−26
Change in WC	7
Capex	−20
FCF	64

Table 7.7 Valuation of new eDreams

Cap Ex structure	
E	58%
D	42%
V	100%
Kd	6%
Ke	12%
t	25%
WACC	8.85%
g	3.77%
EV	1,296

7.3.3 Future challenges

In mid-2014, the new group is facing challenges to implement the business plan and get the profitability expected by the shareholders, estimated at 12%. These challenges are market- as well as company-related.

The main market-related challenges are the consolidation of a shift towards online purchasing, meaning a growth in the OTA market higher than the expected growth in GDP.

In terms of the new group, the main challenges are to get the company successfully integrated, to leverage and strengthen the leading technology platform, and to capitalize the brand value, maintaining attractive margins and generating enough cash.

7.4 Restructuring to sell: the case of Apollo Tyres Ltd

Let's consider this press release:

> Apollo Tyres Ltd. and Cooper Tire & Rubber Company announced the execution of a definitive merger agreement under which a wholly-owned subsidiary of Apollo will acquire Cooper in an all-cash transaction valued at approximately $2.5 billion. The transaction represented a 40% premium to Cooper's 30-day volume-weighted average price.

After reading this announcement one can think that we are back to the *good old days* of the beginning of this century, when the economy was booming and M and A activity represented an important percentage of the GDP.

But we are not. This press release was made on 13 June 2013. Does it make sense that Apollo pays a 40% premium for Cooper? Based on what?

7.4.1 Industry overview

The global automotive tyre industry holds significant opportunities for industry players due to strong demand for replacement tyres and increasing sales of passenger and commercial vehicles in developing countries. The market is forecast to reach an estimated US$ 187 billion in 2017 with a compounded annual growth rate (CAGR) of 4% over the next five years (2012–2017).

Although volatile raw material prices and higher dependency of the suppliers on the original equipment manufacturers (OEMs) are market challenges, the increasing per capita income in developing nations, population growth, new infrastructure projects, urbanization, increase in middle-class population, and the green movement all are expected to drive growth in the industry.

In the global automotive tyre industry, the passenger car segment is forecast to see the highest growth over the next five years. Regionally, the Asia–Pacific (APAC) area is anticipated to experience lead growth during the forecast period. APAC is expected to attain the strongest growth in rubber demand through 2012, reflecting strength in China, India, Thailand and Vietnam.

The global automotive tyre market is highly consolidated and consists of passenger car tyres, heavy truck tyres, and other segments. North America dominates this market with approximately 30% of the global total.

In 2011, Europe emerged as the highest potential market followed by APAC and North America. Competition in the global automotive tyre industry is high. A combination of factors such as vehicle sales, government regulations and environmental factors impacts market dynamics significantly.

7.4.2 Restructuring at Cooper

Prior to this merger, Cooper Tire & Rubber (CT&R) set up an operational restructuring in order to reduce costs and improve efficiency. According to this strategic plan, the company would reduce production costs in 10–15%, by enhancing supply chain coordination, savings in procurement and material usage, control on general expenses and reduction of the complexity on tyre design. CT&R also expected a revenue growth of 6% CAGR, with the introduction of new products, the enhancement of Asian and European products, an improved mix of products and brands and the expansion of the US market.

When Apollo is buying Cooper at 4.75 times EV/EBITDA, it means the company is betting on the synergies associated with the CT&R restructuring and the opportunities coming from access to the US market. In fact, the strategic combination will bring together two companies with highly complementary brands, geographical presence and technological expertise to create a global leader in tyre manufacturing and distribution.

The acquisition augurs well for Apollo Tyres as it would widen its geographical footprint and provide immediate access to two of the world's biggest markets, North America and China. Further, it also provides the company with a manufacturing presence in cost-efficient locations like China and Eastern Europe.

Post-acquisition, the combined entity will be the 7th largest tyre company in the world with combined revenues of US$ 6.6 billion. The combination is expected to deliver value creation benefits of approximately US$ 80–120 million per annum at the EBITDA level. These ongoing benefits are expected to be fully achieved after three years and derived from operating scale, sourcing benefits, technology, product optimization and manufacturing improvements. The transaction is expected to be immediately accretive to Apollo's earnings.

It's interesting to consider that the expected benefits on the EBITDA level would come from the operational restructuring announced in CT&R. Table 7.8 summarizes some expected figures associated to the restructuring process.

Assuming the revenue growth and costs reduction in Cooper associated with the strategic plan, the expected variation of its EBITDA will be from $ 87.3 million to $ 118.7 million. In line with what is expected it will deliver the value creation of the merger. Additionally, if Apollo pays now 4.75 EV/EBITDA ($ 2.5 billion), in 3 years the expected EV of CT&R would be double with a ratio of 6 for the EV/EBITDA ($ 5.0 billion).

7.4.3 The operation

Cooper Chief Executive Roy Armes said of the operation:

> Cooper Tire has been performing well but our stock was undervalued, and Apollo saw the value.

Certainly, the Indian company did. In fact, Apollo decided to finance the acquisition entirely with debt, as an additional way to create value through the capital structure. The company planned to raise $ 2.1 billion of debt by issuing yield bonds (with a duration of 7–8 years) and taking a loan of $ 450 million.

Financing the operation only with debt makes sense, because of the important operational synergies expected and the low financial leverage of Cooper (25% of Debt, in accounting value).

Table 7.8 Cooper Tire & Rubber

Year	2012	2013	2014	2015
Net Sales	4,200,836	4,452,886	4,720,059	5,003,263
EBITDA	525,878	613,174	714,961	833,644
EBITDA as % of Sales	12.5%	13.8%	15.1%	16.7%
EV	2,500,000			5,001,864
EV/EBITDA	4.75			6.00
Variation in EBITDA		87,296	101,787	118,683

7.5 Restructuring to become global: the case of Grupo Silicon

At the end of 2012, the CFO of Grupo Silicon (GS), Carlos Tapia, believed that the company was facing a crucial situation. In the last four years GS had experienced an important growth which was financed basically with new debt. From 2008, the increase of € 6.2 million in total net assets was financed with € 4.5 million of new debt, as shown in Table 7.9.

Mr Tapia was aware that the present business model of growth in GS was not sustainable, since the cash flow generated by its operations was clearly below the company's need for new fixed assets and operational working capital. Moreover, GS had opportunities to invest in new foreign markets (Saudi Arabia, Latin America and some African countries) in the coming years, which will require additional funds. Supporting financial entities were asking for a recovery of their investment.

7.5.1 The company

Grupo Silicon (GS) was founded in 1984 by a group of young entrepreneurs with the goal of providing integrated IS solutions in different fields like security systems, electronics, telecoms, networks, radio telecommunications, audio systems, development of software, electronic war, etc. In 2012 the company was acting in sectors like aeronautics, defence and security, health, education and entertainment.

The company was highly dependent on projects with institutions and companies in the Spanish public sector (Social Security, Ministry of Defence,

Table 7.9 Grupo Silicon balance sheet evolution (Figures in thousands of euros)

Years	2007	2008	2009	2010	2011	2012
Current Assets	17,741.57	15,093.65	16,147.05	17,744.66	18,134.84	16,642.34
Current Liabilities	12,851.48	11,919.37	11,546.11	11,730.38	11,598.00	8,452.18
Net Fixed Assets	2,396.69	2,810.67	3,225.43	3,219.85	3,711.04	4,064.70
Total Net Assets	7,286.77	5,984.94	7,826.38	9,234.13	10,247.88	12,254.86
Debt	2,527.00	1,078.13	2,608.01	3,878.27	4,607.74	5,626.36
Equity	4,759.77	4,906.82	5,218.37	5,355.86	5,640.14	6,628.51
Total D+E	7,286.77	5,984.94	7,826.38	9,234.13	10,247.88	12,254.86

etc.). Due to the economic crisis, the size and profitability of projects in Spain have gone down dramatically in the last few years. GS's management team believed that the future of the company was to become a global player in the international arena, selling its technology and integrated solutions to new foreign markets.

7.5.2 A new business plan

At the end of 2012, GS's management team designed a new business plan in order to make the company both economically viable and profitable. This plan included:

- An aggressive expansion in the new foreign markets. Revenues from external markets would grow from 10% of total Revenues in 2012, to 25% in 2013 and 30% in 2014.
- These new foreign markets would contribute with projects with a higher gross margin.
- A restructuring plan to reduce its operating costs through higher efficiency and reduction in general expenses.
- As a consequence, estimated EBITDA will improve from 10.74% in 2012, to 12.50% in 2017.

Tapia led the negotiations with the supporting financial entities in order to restructure the external financing of Grupo Silicon. He was aware that the banks would ask for specific measures to generate more sustainable cash flow, and they would accept this business plan only if the expected value of the company was higher than the present liquidation value.

Tapia believed that this expected liquidation value for GS was not very high, since the company operated through projects with an important component of intangible value.

At the beginning of 2013, the company started the final negotiations with the banks. As CFO of GS, Tapia presented an aggressive plan to reduce the financial leverage of the company. Table 7.10 summarizes the main elements of this plan.

Note that in this plan the company is assumed to have an excess of cash in hand. Based on the assumption that the needed operational cash in hand was € 500,000, this cash in excess was estimated as € 1,048,650. This amount was dedicated to reduce the amount of debts.

Table 7.10 Expected evolution of some variables according to the Grupo Silicon business plan (Figures of debt in thousands of euros)

Revenues: Annual accumulative increases of 7%
Period: 2013–2017
EBITDA:

Years	2013	2014	2015	2016	2017
EBITDA (% of Revenues)	11.0%	11.5%	12.0%	12.0%	12.5%

Annual Depreciation of 500,000 euros
Corporate tax rate of 30%
Evolution of total Debts:

Years	2012	2013	2014	2015	2016	2017
Debt	4,577.70	4,577.70	2,514.34	785.76	678.85	571.93

Table 7.11 Sensitivity analysis of valuation (Figures in thousands of euros)

TV impact on final Valuation					
g for TV	0.0%	0.5%	1.0%	1.5%	2.0%
EV	16,941.09	17,668.45	18,484.51	19,406.55	20,456.65
E	12,363.39	13,090.75	13,906.81	14,828.85	15,878.95
TV/EBITDA	5.5	5.9	6.2	6.7	7.2

Appendix 7.3 shows in detail the expected evolution of the company's financial statements.

With this business plan, the expected economic value of GS (EV) was around €17,000,000, 8.5 times EBITDA, when the accounting value was €12,255,000. This was a conservative evaluation, since the expected Terminal Value was supposed to be 5.5 times EBITDA.[3]

Table 7.11 summarizes a sensitivity analysis of the expected value of GS.

Appendix 7.4 includes a detailed explanation of the evaluation made for GS.

The management team of GS was confident of getting the support from the banks for this business plan. By implementing these changes, the company will become economically feasible and profitable. Furthermore, in a conservative scenario, the expected economic value of GS will be 38.2% higher than the present accounting value, in a context of a present liquidation value likely lower than the accounting value.

Appendices

Appendix 7.1 Assumptions to evaluate Foster's in a conservative scenario

Years	2012	2013	2014	2015	2016
Evolution of P&L					
Variation in Revenue	3.0%	3.5%	3.5%	3.5%	3.5%
Cost of sales (% of Revenues)	49.5%	49.0%	48.5%	48.0%	48.0%
Gross Margin (As a percentage of Revenues)					
Selling exp.	7.0%	7.0%	7.0%	7.0%	7.0%
Marketing exp.	5.0%	5.0%	5.0%	5.0%	5.0%
Admin exp.	2.0%	2.0%	2.0%	2.0%	2.0%
Other exp.	2.0%	2.0%	2.0%	2.0%	2.0%
EBITDA (As a percentage of Revenues)					
Depreciation and amortization	3.0%	3.0%	3.0%	3.0%	3.0%
Estimated Evolution of Operational WC					
Cash in hand (days of sales)	8	7	6	5	5
Acc. receivables (days of sales)	75	70	65	60	60
Inventories (days of CofGS)	45	40	35	30	30
Acc payables (days of CofGS)	145	130	110	90	90

Investments in Capex equal to 5% of Revenues

Terminal Value of E will be the same as the present price, meaning 14.3 times EBITDA.

Appendix 7.2 Additional information on the Foster's acquisition

Source: Independent expert's report (Grant Samuel, Appendix 1).

SABMiller

Company introduction. SABMiller is the world's second largest brewing company in sales. The Company has South African origins (19th century) but has grown, both organically and through acquisitions, to have a global footprint and reach the size it has now. Their brand portfolio includes more than 200 different brands, out of which Grolsch, Miller, Peroni Nastro Azzurro and Pilsner Urquell, are the most notable. The company has more than 70,000 employees, is present in more than 75 countries in all continents, generates sales of over US$ 28 billion and a profit before tax in FY2011 of over US$ 3.5 billion.[4]

Company's strategy. SABMiller can be distinguished from the other multinational brewers for: (i) being best positioned to take advantage of the growth that recently has spurted in emerging markets (mostly Latin America, Africa and Asia),[5] and (ii) focus on local brands, their history and heritage, and reinforcing their consumer's loyalty. The acquisition of local brands in emerging countries is considered to be the major factor driving shareholder value creation in the last decade for SABMiller. Additionally, although most of the sales in the industry are related with local (national) brands, the imported beers segment is also growing considerably, mostly in developed countries. This is why SABMiller is also developing a range of global brands that appeal to the taste of sophisticated individuals that are willing to pay the corresponding premium in their price. Parallel to this revenue side strategy, the Company has been implementing very effective global synergies and cost savings programmes that have succeeded in considerable EBITA increases in saturated markets (Europe and the US). Finally, SABMiller has also been an active player in the industry consolidation.

Recent M and A history. SABMiller was until 1990 a South African brewery. But then it started to invest in Europe: Hungarian Dreher in 1993, Polish Lech in 1995, several Romanian breweries in 1996, Slovakian Pivovar Saris in 1997, Russian Kaluga in 1998 and several Czech and Polish breweries in 1999. By this time, the company had raised a significant amount of equity while moving its listing to London, in order to finance further acquisitions. They then moved into the Indian market, entered South and Central American markets and further expanded in other African countries. A first major deal occurred in 2002 with the acquisition of Miller Brewing Company, which led the change in the name of the company, thus becoming the second largest brewer in the world in volume. The major deals that followed were: Italian Birra Peroni in 2003, South American Bavaria in 2005, several breweries in China in 2006 that made it the largest brewer in China, and Dutch Grolsch in 2008. Throughout this period, SABMiller also made plenty of other acquisitions in different regions of the world. In addition, it also signed joint-venture agreements with some major players (e.g. Molson) to launch their beers in emerging countries. It also acquired Foster's business in some countries (e.g. India) while signing licensed-brewing partnerships with that same company in other major markets (the US). These deals with Foster's might have been motivation for the real deal that took place this year, and the brands of Foster's might be one reason for the acquisition.

Multiples analysis vs peers. When analysing a transaction, one of the necessary first steps is to analyse the acquirer. SABMiller, according to Morningstar data, is trading at a very low EV/EBITDA multiple compared to

Peers' comparable multiples

2010	EBITDA Margin	D/E (cap)	Total debt (mill)	Total cap	Currency	EV	Net margin	Net income	Revenues	EBITDA	EV/EBITDA
AB InBev	38%	56%	44,894	80,168	USD	125,062	12%	4,227	36,128	13,873	9.01
Carlsberg	24%	42%	37,241	89,737	DKK	126,978	9%	5,545	60,272	14,284	8.89
Heineken	20%	47%	9,072	19,302	EUR	28,374	12%	2,252	18,924	3,804	7.46
Molson Coors	34%	20%	1961	9,756	USD	11,717	21%	686	3,251	1,105	10.6
	29%	41%					13%				8.99
SABMiller	35%	28%	8,460	30,432	USD	38,892	16%	2,408	15,145	5,255	7.40

Source: Morningstar.

its main peers in the industry (for FY2010). As of March 2011, UBS estimated a 9.1× for that multiple, much closer to the industry average. What is more relevant to consider is the low leverage of SABMiller, giving it a relevant margin for additional acquisitions financed with debt.

The beer industry worldwide

Main players. The industry is dominated by AB InBev with 25% of global market share. The top five is completed by SABMiller, Carlsberg, Heineken and MolsonCoors. In the last decade, all these players have made considerable acquisitions in the industry, thus reaching, all together, more than 50% of global market share.

Consolidation in the industry. Especially in Europe and in the US, beer sales growth has been consistently reducing, with even a decline being recorded in some countries, in favour of wines and spirits.[6] This has led the major players in the industry to focus on synergies and cost savings in order to compensate for the reduction in sales with higher operational margins. However, most of these synergies and cost savings could not be generated without further increasing size and bargaining power, as most of them can only be derived from the relationships with suppliers, distributors and retailers. These were the drivers for consolidation in the industry: (i) gain more bargaining power in procurement; (ii) optimization of production capacity and distribution; (iii) control the brands' placement at the retailer; (iv) optimize the brand portfolio management and pricing.

Another factor that has driven consolidation is the asymmetric growth prospects in different regions in the world. Basically, the underdeveloped world has been recording significant GDP growth in the last decade which has driven beer consumption to very high growth levels. Having exposure to these markets has been a major concern for every brewery, and huge acquisitions have taken place in the past (e.g. InBev acquiring Brazilian giant Brahma for US$ 11.2 billion). Additionally, taking advantage of complementary geographical presence/domination in emerging markets has also been another driver for consolidation (e.g. InBev acquiring US giant Anheuser-Busch for US$ 52 billion), which generate instant savings in marketing expenses that were allocated to gain market share.[7]

Both factors explained above are expected to continue driving consolidation, and if AB InBev, SABMiller, Carlsberg and Heineken already account for approximately 50% of beer consumption in the world, during this decade, with their investment in the emerging countries and further consolidation of local players, it is expected to account for much more, thus displaying a global oligopoly in the beer industry.

Factors of competitive advantage. All of what has been said before is consistent with affirming that size matters in the beer industry. From many points of view, size does affect the ability companies have to optimize their revenue generation, production capacity and distribution network, and gain power in procurement. The rise of global brands and the deep marketing and distribution expertise have given the major players in the industry a competitive advantage over any local players. It becomes evident to smaller breweries' shareholders that value creation is maximized through taking part in the consolidation process. Even though the recent past has shown that M and A transactions in this industry are not creating much value, we should always compare it with the scenario where consolidation wouldn't have taken place: the big players in the developed world would be condemned to markets of declining consumption and few alternatives to generate cost savings.

SABMiller acquisition of Foster's

SABMiller's rationale. SABMiller's rationale for acquiring Foster was published on its website,[8] and their main reasons were:
Strong country and industry fundamentals: Australia is a country with a growing population and good GDP growth prospects, it's a very profitable beer market and Foster's has a leading market share competing with only one other player.

- Opportunity to improve performance: generating synergies from its global scale and implementing SABMiller best practices to drive extra EBITDA.
- Financial opportunity: both companies are under-leveraged compared to the industry average, a reason why the acquisition will allow the combined company to approximate the estimated optimal capital structure and thus enhance its enterprise value.

Foster's – company analysis. The Australian beer market compares with the Canadian market in terms of growth prospects and profitability. That is why the multiples of Foster and Molson are quite similar. The EV/EBITDA multiple above industry average is mostly justified by a lower risk profile of the countries where most of the sales are generated (North America and Australia), the low currency exchange risk, and perhaps the fact that it already includes a potential premium anticipating that these companies

Peers' comparable multiples

2010	EBITDA Margin	D/E (cap)	Total Debt (mill)	Total cap	Currency	EV	Net margin	Net income	Revenues	EBITDA	EV/ EBITDA
AB InBev	38%	56%	44,894	80,168	USD	125,062	12%	4,227	36,128	13,873	9.01
Carlsberg	24%	42%	37,241	89,737	DKK	126,978	9%	5,545	60,272	14,284	8.89
Heineken	20%	47%	9,072	19,302	EUR	28,374	12%	2,252	18,924	3,804	7.46
Molson Coors	34%	20%	1961	9,756	USD	11,717	21%	686	3,251	1,105	10.6
	29%	41%									
SABMiller	35%	28%	8,46	30,432	USD	38,892	16%	2,408	15,145	5,255	7.4
Source: Morningstar											
Foster's (1)	40%	27%	2185	8,029	AUD	10,214	23%	542	2395	951	10.74

Source: Foster's 2011 Annual Report – 2010 figures. From continuing operations.

are good acquisition targets by the main players in the industry. Judging from this data set, and considering that Foster's EBITDA margin is quite well above the industry average, we can already begin questioning if there are potential additional operating efficiencies to be achieved by SABMiller with Foster's. We can therefore reasonably conclude that cost savings is not the actual reason behind the acquisition of this company.

The transaction. On 21 September 2011, Foster's Board of Directors accepted an offer from SABMiller for A$5.1 per share paid in cash, pending approval by its shareholders. This price implies the following valuation of Foster's of A$11.5 billion (enterprise value) and an EV/EBITDA multiple of 13×.

Analysis of the transaction using comparable peers' multiples. Judging from the peers' multiples in the market, the premium paid in the EV is close to 4× EBITDA. Even though this figure might seem very high, we also need to consider the strategic position of the target: market leader in a duopoly and a very profitable market.

Analysis of the transaction using comparable transaction multiples. The major comparable transactions occurred in mature markets (sourced from UBS) and corresponding relevant averages are as follows:

Peers' comparable transactions

Date	Target	Acquirer	Country	EV/ EBITDA	Notes
Aug-09	Tennent's	C&C	UK	8.2	Excluded
Aug-09	Lion Nathan	Kirin	Australia	12.5	Main reference in the market
Jul-08	Anheuser-Busch	InBev	US	12.4	(A)
Jan-08	Scottish & Newcastle	Heineken	UK	11.9	(A)
Jan-08	Scottish & Newcastle	Carlsberg	UK	13.9	(A)
Nov-07	Grolsch	SABMiller	Netherlands	14.6	(A)
Aug-05	Belhaven Group	Greene King	UK	11.1	
May-05	Mahou San Miguel	Mahou	Spain	9.5	
Feb-05	Birra Peroni	SABMiller	Italy	20.0	Excluded
Jul-04	Molson	Coors	Canada	10.4	(A)
May-04	Licher&Koenig	Bitburger	Germany	9.0	
Feb-04	Carlsberg Breweries	Carlsberg	Denmark	9.5	
Feb-04	Brau&Brunnen	Dr Oetker	Germany	3.7	Excluded
Jan-04	Holsten	Carlsberg	Germany	9.1	
Sep-03	Apatinska	Interbrew	Germany	6.3	Excluded
May-03	Birra Peroni	SABMiller	Italy	12.6	(A)
			Average	**11.4**	
			Average (2008/09)	**12.7**	
			SABMiller's average	**13.6**	
			(A) Most relevant comparable transactions	**13.1**	

There are different multiples we can compare this transaction with: (i) a relevant transaction happened in Australia 2 years ago with a multiple of 12.5×: this means that the 13× multiple in this transaction is not that high; (ii) the average of relevant comparable transactions in the last years (2008/2009) is also pretty close to this transactions' multiple – 12.7×, and considering a larger period, the multiple in comparable transactions even exceeds that of this transaction – 13.1×; (iii) finally, SABMiller seems to have a practice of paying a multiple above the industry average – 13.6×, which in the process of negotiations should be acting against them. Overall, based on multiples of comparable transactions, the price paid for Foster's seems to be close to the higher end of the range but is still within the reasonable range of prices paid in previous transactions.

Final considerations

SABMiller's acquisition of Foster's can be mainly justified by a need to continue growing and eliminate the possibility of its competitors becoming bigger and catching one of the remaining medium players in the market susceptible to acquisition. The option to acquire Foster's needs to be analysed against a possible scenario of it being acquired by a competitor, and thus SABMiller losing relative power in the overall global market and losing the option to enhance and optimize its global presence.

It seems to me that this transaction has a very interesting reasoning from the point of view of capital structure analysis: both companies were under-leveraged compared to the industry average, and the acquisition by SABMiller should enable the combined company to reach an enterprise value higher than the algebraic sum of both companies, because the capital structure becomes closer to its optimal combination. On the other hand there are other factors that seem to point to this transaction creating value for SABMiller's shareholders: (i) increasing a portfolio of global brands that could be used to further enhance the brand portfolio in the premium segment in several countries; (ii) diversifying SABMiller's geographical exposure which was highly concentrated in emerging and developing markets, by adding one of the few developed markets that is not suffering in the current government debt/economic crisis; (iii) SABMiller already had some investments in Australia which can be consolidated with Foster's and thus generate some cost savings; (iv) a stronger presence in Australia might be a starting point to further increase the group's presence and market share in Southeast Asia; v) finally, the 'Foster's' beer brand will be shared worldwide with Heineken (Europe – owned) and Molson (Canada – license agreement), and SABMiller will own the brand directly in US, Australia and Asia, which might create an opportunity to consolidate the brand should the company be able to acquire the rights in Europe at a reasonable price and the licensing agreement be close to an end. All-in-all, I do believe that this transaction makes sense for SABMiller from a strategic point of view. In an industry that is consolidating, it's a seller's market, and therefore the prices paid are high.[9] However, history has shown that in each country the main players are relatively stable with a high level of loyalty from consumers to local national brands. The opportunity seems to come from the increase in the premium imported beers segment, where Australian brands, from a country known for its special thirst for beer, could easily become global brands and be introduced or developed in several other markets.

For Foster's shareholders, considering the company doesn't have the size, and has already lost the opportunity to grow and to make considerable and relevant acquisitions, the remaining option is get the best price for their shares. The implied EV/EBITDA multiple seems to value the company in the higher range of other comparable transactions and it seems to signal that they are getting a good price for their shares.

Appendix 7.3 Forecast financial statements of Grupo Silicon

Operational Profit and Loss

Years	2013	2014	2015	2016	2017
Revenues	19,926.18	21,321.01	22,813.48	24,410.43	26,119.16
EBITDA	2,191.88	2,451.92	2,737.62	2,929.25	3,264.89
Depreciation	−500.00	−500.00	−500.00	−500.00	−500.00
EBIT	1,691.88	1,951.92	2,237.62	2,429.25	2,764.89
Taxes on EBIT	−507.56	−585.57	−671.29	−728.78	−829.47
EBIaT	1,184.32	1,366.34	1,566.33	1,700.48	1,935.43
FCF from Operations	1,684.32	1,866.34	2,066.33	2,200.48	2,435.43

Balance Sheet

Years	2012	2013	2014	2015	2016	2017
Curr. Assets (cash=500)	15593.68	16685.24	17853.21	19102.93	20440.14	21870.95
Current Lab.	8452.18	9043.83	9676.9	10354.29	11079.09	11854.62
Net Curr. Assets	7141.50	7641.41	8176.31	8748.65	9361.05	10016.33
Net Fixed Assets	4064.7	3702.05	3340.69	2980.45	2621.2	2262.98
Total Net Assets	11206.21	11343.45	11516.99	11729.09	11982.25	12279.31
Debt	4577.7	4577.7	2514.34	785.76	678.85	571.93
Equity	6628.5	6765.75	9002.65	10943.33	11303.4	11707.38
Total L+E	11206.21	11343.45	11516.99	11729.09	11982.25	12279.31

Appendix 7.4 Valuation of Grupo Silicon

Years	2012	2013E	2014E	2015E	2016E	2017E
E	12363.39	12758.17	15106.89	17038.28	17317.65	17424.56
D	4577.7	4577.7	2514.34	785.76	678.85	571.93
V	16941.09	17335.87	17621.24	17824.04	17996.5	17996.49
Beta u	0.7					
Rf	5.00%					
MP	6%					
Ke,u	9.20%	9.20%	9.20%	9.20%	9.20%	9.20%
Kd	8.50%	8.50%	8.50%	8.50%	8.50%	8.50%
Ke,l		9.46%	9.45%	9.32%	9.23%	9.23%
WACC		8.51%	8.53%	8.84%	9.09%	9.10%
FCF		1047.07	1192.80	1354.23	1447.32	1638.37
TV						17996.49
FCF to disc		1047.07	1192.80	1354.23	1447.32	19634.86
Fact of discount		1.085	1.178	1.282	1.398	1.53
FCF at PV		964.94	1012.88	1056.6	1035.16	12871.51
EV	16941.09					
ECF		774.7	-1142.93	-523.96	1293.66	1491.06
TV						17424.56
ECF to disc		774.7	-1142.93	-523.96	1293.66	18915.63
Disc factor		1.095	1.198	1.31	1.431	1.563
ECF at PV		707.75	-954.00	-400.07	904.29	12105.41
E	12363.39					
#Acc	1000.00					
Price	12.36					

8
Life after Restructuring

8.1 Chapter overview

The quality of a proposed restructuring can be analysed in terms of the following points:

- Fairness
- Stability
- Company viability
- Company value generation opportunities.

In order to be permanent, a restructuring agreement must be fair. The negotiations should produce agreements resulting in win–win solutions for all the parties involved. The expected evolution of the company should be sustainable, based on realistic assumptions. How to know when the assumptions are realistic? By being specific in identifying who will do what, when, how and through what means.

The quality of any restructuring process depends on how the business plan captures and reflects the key value drivers of the company, pointing out its future opportunities and adapting the company to reach its objectives accordingly, not only in its operational aspects but in its future capital structure as well.

8.2 Introduction

In the preceding chapters we have discussed how to implement the restructuring process of a company, the steps we should follow and pitfalls to avoid. We also learned some lessons from actual examples of actual restructurings.

Let's now consider the case of Arsys, a leading company in web hosting and cloud services. The company was founded in 1996 by two friends and, in December 2007, the founders sold it to Carlyle and Mercapital, two private equity funds. The buyers paid for the Equity a price of € 200 million, equivalent to 5 times expected revenues and 20 times expected EBITDA, reflecting a significant expected growth in the coming years. Arsys' revenues have remained constant since 2008, around € 40 million per year. In August 2013 Arsys was sold to its main competitor, United Internet, for € 140 million, an exit price clearly below the estimated price in its 2007 business plan. How could that be? Among other reasons, this was due to Arsys' loss of market share, since Arsys was unable to increase revenues in a market that was experiencing an annual average rate of growth of 10% during the last four years.

Can we prevent these kinds of situations? How could we avoid overestimating positive synergies, and/or underestimating negative ones?

In this chapter, we'll deal with the company's life after a restructuring. Basically, we'll try to answer the following question: Is the completion of a restructuring process in a company a guarantee of future success?

8.3 Quality of the restructuring: the day after

As we know, restructuring is about fixing problems. Some people believe that a way to solve problems is to do nothing. By doing nothing you might solve the problem, but it is not normally the best way of going about it. Even worse than doing nothing is doing it badly.

How could we know whether the restructuring process is enough to solve the cash flow problems? We can address this by analysing the quality of the proposed restructuring, in the context of the following points:

- Fairness
- Stability
- Company viability
- Company value generation opportunities.

8.3.1 Fairness

In order to be permanent, any agreement should be fair. In any restructuring there are a lot of negotiations among different parties. These negotiations should end in agreements based on win–win solutions: one party gains not because the other party loses, but because everyone gains.[1]

In Chapter 1 we already mentioned how difficult can it be to share the needed sacrifices in a restructuring process among all the parties involved.

These should consider accepting the proposed agreements as a way to move from a situation where loss is the order of the day to a situation whereby all parties stand to gain, at least in relative terms.

8.3.2 Stability

The expected evolution in the company in question should be sustainable, based on realistic assumptions. How to know if some assumptions are realistic? Being specific is the best way: identify who is going to do what, clarify when, how and using what means.

At the end of the day, the refinancing associated with any restructuring is possible because the supporting financial entities believe in the future of the company as detailed in the new business plan. To be successful in selling a business plan we must be aware that sustainable changes don't occur overnight. Dramatic changes might appear and they might be positive or negative. In any case, do we have a realistic plan B for crises?

Another important issue to be discussed is the size and composition of the Capex. It's very useful to separate Capex for maintenance and Capex for growth. Both of these should be consistent with the new strategy designed for the company.

8.3.3 Company viability

In Chapter 2 we defined the Net Cash Flow of a company as the liquidity generated from all of its operational activities (including interest expenses) and from its Equity. The best way to analyse the economic feasibility of a company is to understand the amount and composition of the Net Cash Flow (NCF) that the company is generating. We should bear in mind that:

- Debt amortization or reduction is only achieved by generating positive net cash flow (NCF).
- A company in a permanent state of negative NCF is economically unsustainable.
- The total short-term liquidity generated by a company is the sum of its Net Cash Flow coming from short-term operating activities (P and L and WC), while the long-term liquidity is the sum of its Net Cash Flow generated by Investments in FA (Capex) and Capital.
- We must know whether the problem is caused by a short- or long-term liquidity shortage, and whether it is recurrent or not, in order to understand the company's liquidity problems. Accordingly, short-term problems call for different solutions than long-term ones. The former tend to be recurrent, whereas the latter can be temporary or associated with

particular phases in the life of the business. The former would need short-term finance, and the latter should be financed from long-term borrowings.

- It is not just a matter of generating a positive NCF, but also analysing its sustainability over time. In this regard, the situation of Publications, Inc. would be very different if the imbalance between liquidity generated from short-term and long-term sources was a temporary condition or a permanent one.
- In the hypothetical situation of a permanently self-financing company, the liquidity generated in the short-term would be the amount used to finance long-term policies, that is, its investments and return on capital; its NCF would be zero.

Consider the case of 3 companies with a profile of NCF as detailed in Table 8.1.

Note in the example that the three companies are each generating € 30 million in NCF. It is clear that company A shows a more sustainable profile in terms of liquidity, since there is a balance between short-term liquidity (€ 150 million), long-term investments (Capex) and redistribution to its investors (shareholders and financial entities). Conversely, in company B we have a problem with shareholders' redistribution, providing the company only needs €20 million in Capex. Finally, NCF generated by company C is most likely unsustainable, since there is not positive liquidity generated by short-term activities, and the positive € 30 million of NCF comes from new funds from shareholders and no investment in Capex.

8.3.4 Company value generation opportunities

Through the analysis of the NCF of a company we can differentiate the short-term and long-term liquidity (positive or negative) that it generates. Accordingly, we can analyse the composition of its debt in terms of maturity (short-term/ long-term).

Table 8.1 Net Cash Flow composition (Figures in million euros)

	Company A	Company B	Company C
Cash from operations (P and L)	200	100	50
Cash from Operational WC	–50	–50	–50
Cash from Capex	–100	–20	0
Cash from shareholders	–20	0	30
Total NCF	30	30	30

As we already explained in Chapter 1, the Free Cash Flow (FCF) summarizes the money generated through the operating activities of a company (resulting from the management of all its operational aspects included in the Profit and Loss and Operational Assets). A company will only ensure its continuity by generating enough FCF to remain feasible and to compensate shareholders with money that will satisfy their expected goal of economic profitability. In any company, economic sustainability means that the company will generate enough FCF to be feasible and profitable. Consequently, understanding how a company generates FCF is the best way to decide what the capital structure of that company should be, subject to a given level of risk and expected profitability.[2]

The quality of any restructuring process will depend on how the business plan captures and reflects the key value drivers for the company, specifying its future opportunities and how to adapt the company to achieve its objectives, not only in its operational side but in its future capital structure as well.

8.4 Revisiting Publications, Inc.

Let's now apply these considerations to the case of Publications, Inc. introduced earlier in Chapter 1. Let's keep in mind that Publications, Inc. is a multimedia company that provides e-learning services. It operates in Germany and it is facing a very delicate condition in terms of liquidity. At the end of 2013, Tables 8.2 and 8.3 show a summary of the financial situation of the company.

Table 8.2 Publications, Inc., 2013 (Figures in thousands of euros)

		As a % of Revenues
Revenues	10,856	
EBIT	221	2.0%
Taxes on EBIT	–55	
EBIaT	166	1.5%
Depreciation	327	3.0%
FCF from P&L	493	
FCF from Operational WC	474	
FCF from Capex	–850	
Total FCF	117	
The Balance Sheet is:		
Net Current Assets	1,322	
Net Fixed Assets	5,058	
Total Net Assets	6,380	
Total Debt	4,257	
EQUITY	2,123	
Total D + E	6,380	

Table 8.3 Publications, Inc.: summary of NCF evolution (Figures in thousands of euros)

Years	2008	2009	2010	2011	2012	2013	Total period
Net Earnings	347	340	211	132	85	8	1,123
Depreciation	333	324	325	346	363	327	2,018
Net Cash Flow from P&L	680	664	536	478	448	335	3,141
Variation in Operat WC	222	−246	−624	143	−491	474	−522
Variation in Capex	−1,368	−1,221	−1,435	−684	−338	−850	−5,896
Variation in Equity	0	0	0	0	0	0	0
Total Net Cash Flow	−466	−803	−1,523	−63	−381	−41	−3,277
Variation in Debt	466	803	1523	63	381	41	3,277

As discussed in Chapter 2, during 2008–2013 that company generated € 2.6 million from its short-term activities, and only invested € 5.9 million in Capex, with no redistribution to its shareholders. This imbalance between short-term generation of liquidity and long-term investments produced a negative NCF of € 3.3 million which was financed by a corresponding increase in Debt of € 3.3 million. Its current outstanding Debt (€ 4.3 million) is made up of € 3.5 million in short-term financing and € 0.8 million in long-term debt.

It's clear that the condition of Publications, Inc. is unsustainable. To survive, the company urgently needs to generate liquidity from operational (short-term) activities and to reduce dramatically the investments in Capex. It also needs a more reasonable balance between short-term financing and long-term needs.

After long negotiations with its supporting financial entities, the current shareholders of Publications, Inc. have presented a plan for the restructuring of the company that includes the following points:

1) Appointment of a new management team. This new management team includes experienced managers with an excellent reputation in the industry and familiar with these types of restructuring for similar companies.
2) No dividends or other kind of redistribution will be paid to the shareholders in the coming five years.
3) Outstanding debt will be restructured, by converting 80% of its total debt into a long-term syndicated loan, and the remaining 20% into short-term revolving credit. The average estimated cost of the new debt will be 4%.
4) Investments in Capex will be limited to maintenance and business continuity, with an estimated annual amount of € 500,000.

5) The new management team will be responsible for implementing important operational improvements, as reflected in Table 8.4. These improvements will come from:
   a) Focusing sales in new markets with higher margins (executive education, for example).
   b) Controlling general expenses.
   c) Increasing efficiency by implementing new IT tools.
   d) More efficient management of operational working capital, especially in collection activities.

Assuming that the new business plan is implemented, what are the expected changes in Publications, Inc?

Table 8.5 summarizes the projected evolution of the liquidity of Publications according to the new business plan and financing restructure.[3]

Clearly, with this business plan the company's objective is to balance the liquidity generated from operational activities (€ 2.8 million) with the long-term investments needed in Capex (€ 2.5 million). This is expected to

Table 8.4 Expected operational improvements

Years	2014	2015	2016	2017	2018
Revenues (expected annual increase)	3.0%	3.0%	3.5%	4.0%	4.5%
EBIT (as a % of Revenues)	2.0%	2.5%	3.0%	3.5%	4.0%
Taxes on EBIT/EBT	25.0%	22.5%	20.0%	20.0%	20.0%
Depreciation (as a % of Revenues)	3.0%	3.0%	3.0%	3.0%	3.0%
Net Current Assets (as % Revenues)	12.0%	11.0%	10.0%	9.0%	8.0%

Table 8.5 Projected evolution of liquidity

Years	2014	2015	2016	2017	2018	Total period
Net Earnings	40	87	146	209	282	763
Depreciation	337	347	359	373	390	1,806
Net Cash Flow from P and L	377	434	505	583	672	2,570
Variation in Operating WC	–20	75	75	76	79	286
Variation in Capex	–500	–500	–500	–500	–500	–2,500
Variation in Equity	0	0	0	0	0	0
Total Net Cash Flow	–143	9	79	159	251	355
Variation in Debt	143	–9	–79	–159	–251	–355

occur (eventually) in 2016 and after fixing the imbalance the company will be able to rethink its strategy in terms of future growth and new suitable capital structure.

How realistic is this plan? Does it make any sense? Can it be accepted by the supporting financial entities? Let's now analyse the quality of this restructuring in terms of the foregoing points.

The business plan appears to be fair since all participants will have to share sacrifices: management team and employees will have to become more efficient, shareholders will have to wait for compensation, supporting financial entities will keep their financing to avoid a liquidation of the company and the associated losses. Implementation of such business plan will provide stability to the company, reducing the ratio of debt to equity (in accounting terms) from the present 2.01 to 1.35 in five years. Furthermore, it is expected that the company will start generating positive FCF and NCF in 2015 (see Appendix 8.1).

Publications, Inc. will only be viable if the financial entities agree to the restructuring of its debt, converting 80% into long-term debt and allowing revolving credit for the rest. Why would these banks do that? Because they believe in the business plan, and the value of the company according to this business plan will be higher than the current liquidation value of the company.

The current liquidation value of Publications, Inc. would most probably lead to losses for the banks because the liquidation value of its assets would be lower than the total amount of its outstanding debt. On the other hand, the economic value of Publications, Inc. associated with the business plan can be estimated as € 10.2 million, assuming a terminal value (TV) equivalent to 8.5 times for the ratio E/EBITDA.[4]

In summary, provided that the new management team is able to implement the expected changes, this restructuring plan will be a win–win solution. Table 8.6 contains the results of a sensitivity analysis on some key variables of this win–win situation.

We can appreciate that a change in the operational assumptions – no improvement in percentage increase in Revenues, lower than expected improvements in EBIT and operational working capital – might lead to a situation where the revolving credit will remain practically unchanged (from € 851,000 to € 823,000), financial leverage will be higher (ratio of E/D of 0.62 instead of 0.74) and the EV of Publications, Inc will be € 9.2 million instead of € 10.2 million.

Table 8.6 Sensitivity analysis

Base Scenario
Debt Evolution

Years	**2013**	**2014**	**2015**	**2016**	**2017**	**2018**
Revolving Credit	851	994	986	906	748	496
Syndicated Loan	3,406	3,406	3,406	3,406	3,406	3,406
Total Debt	4,257	4,400	4,392	4,312	4,153	3,902
Ratio Coverage of Debt		1.00	1.00	1.00	1.00	1.00
E/D in accounting value		0.49	0.51	0.56	0.63	0.74
EV	10,196					
TV	8.50 times E/EBITDA					

Modified scenario
Bad case scenario in operational terms

Years	**2014**	**2015**	**2016**	**2017**	**2018**
Revenues (expected annual increase)	3.00%	3.00%	3.00%	3.00%	3.00%
EBIT (as a % of Revenues)	2.00%	2.30%	2.50%	2.80%	3.00%
Taxes on EBIT/EBT	25.00%	22.50%	20.00%	20.00%	20.00%
Depreciation (as a % of Revenues)	3.00%	3.00%	3.00%	3.00%	3.00%
Net Current Assets (as % Revenues)	12.00%	11.50%	10.50%	9.50%	8.50%

Debt Evolution

Years	**2013**	**2014**	**2015**	**2016**	**2017**	**2018**
Revolving credit	851	994	1,066	1,035	956	823
Syndicated Loan	3,406	3,406	3,406	3,406	3,406	3,406
Total Debt	4,257	4,400	4,471	4,441	4,362	4,229
Ratio Coverage of Debt		1.00	1.00	1.00	1.00	1.00
E/D in accounting value		0.49	0.5	0.52	0.56	0.62
EV	9,180					
TV	8.50 times E/EBITDA					

8.5 Lessons learned from the crises

The first lesson to be learned from any crisis is that crises do happen. Therefore, if you are facing a management decision, it would not be realistic to take decisions based on the wishful assumption that the economy will continue to grow forever.

Precisely, this is the type of behaviour that has led the companies to the present crisis.

The second lesson is to be realistic. How can we do that? By understanding the industry (or business) where we are investing, and the limitations of the tools we are using for our analysis. At the end of the day, we should have reasonable answers to questions like:

- Who is going to do it?
- What is she going to do?
- How is she going to do it?
- With what resources?

Another way of being realistic is having a plan B ready. Not only in the event of future bad news, but also for future good news. What is your limit for stopping losses or your limit for expansion, if needed?

The third lesson is to work closely with your investment partners. In a restructuring, investors are not only shareholders, but also your supporting financial entities. Be a step ahead by preparing the (eventual) next round. Be transparent. Communicate effectively.

More lessons: in times of crisis like the one we are facing, companies are encouraged to go 'back to basics'. That advice is very useful providing that:

1) companies know what are their basics; and
2) companies have good basics.

Which leads us to the central key question: what is a good basic in a company? How can we know if a company is grounded in good basics? The answer is neither easy, nor simple, since there are several factors to take into consideration: type of industry, sustainable competitive advantages, management team profile, external conditions, etc.

Without the intention of being exhaustive, let me share with you some elements I believe should be considered in the identification of the good basics in any company:

1) Management is about taking decisions and implementing them but basing those decisions on the expected economic value, not only on the accounting value.
2) Resources used have a cost.
3) Do not forget the risk associated with any business decision.

4) Expectations depend on external and internal factors. To improve expectations through internal factors we have to generate confidence, which means delivering.
5) Growth does not necessarily mean economic value creation.
6) Know the economic profitability of your customers, not only the accounting profitability.
7) Reward management according to the economic value it has created, not only for the accounting profit.
8) With the short-term outlook, focus on economic feasibility. With a long-term perspective, look for economic value and economic profitability.

As mentioned in a classic textbook on valuation:[5]

> Becoming a value manager is not a mysterious process that is open to only a few. It does require, however, a different perspective from that taken by many managers. It requires a focus on long run cash flows returns, not quarter-to-quarter changes in earnings per share.

More supporting quotation:

> This lowering of the objectives of global finance to the very short term reduces its capacity to function as a bridge between the present and the future, and as a stimulus to the creation of new opportunities for production and for work in the long term. Finance limited in this way to the short and very short term becomes dangerous for everyone, even for those who benefit when the markets perform well.

Who would you guess is the author of this paragraph? In what kind of document is it included? What about a finance professor in a finance textbook? Would you buy that this is the talk of a business guru explaining the present crisis?

Good tries, but the answers are no.

Let me provide you with some more hints:

> In a modern economy, the value of assets is utterly dependent on the capacity to generate revenue in the present and the future. Wealth creation therefore becomes an inescapable duty, which must be kept in mind if the fight against material poverty is to be effective in the long term.

Now you believe you got it! Present value, economic value creation, short-term vs long-term, markets performance, etc, etc. This must be...

Well, think twice.[6]

Finally, let's make some considerations about the future.

In times of crisis, with almost everybody panicking, sharp and cool-headed investors used to step in and make a fortune. Ultimately, it's a matter of following a rule as simple as that: buy low, sell high.

The question is: when is it really low? When is it low enough?

Some hints: it's low when the prices in capital markets are at an historical low (for example, FTSE 100 and IBEX 35 indexes having a historical low price–earnings ratio); and when the yields of bonds rated BBB (the lowest to qualify for investment grade) are at an historical high in comparison with government bonds.

Other useful information is to look at the evolution of investors' confidence. Global Investor Confidence is an index that measures investor confidence on a quantitative basis by analysing the actual buying and selling patterns of institutional investors. The more of their portfolio that institutional investors are willing to devote to equities, the greater their confidence or appetite for risk.

At the end of the day, reasonability of personal decisions depends on realistic alternatives being available, and on logical expectations. In any case, it is important to distinguish between being brave and being stupid. In most cases, information makes the difference.

And a final question: do we need a new financial system? I don't believe we do. What I do believe is that we need a better use and application of the present financial system, refocusing traditional ideas and new ways for innovation.

As already commented, perhaps the most difficult task in management is to reconcile short-term activities with long-term outlook. In that sense, proposed reforms to the financial system should take into account the following guidelines:

1) Reward sustainable economic value creation versus generation of apparent profitability measured through convenient shortcuts.
2) Define and implement effective tools to measure systematic risk.
3) Increase regulation in order to improve transparency in the information provided by financial entities. Greater transparency is needed in areas such as:
   - the use of off-balance sheet entities to hide risky and unclear positions;
   - the standardization of derivative products and higher transparency of these products by trading them in organized markets;

- the definition of internal credit rating procedures in financial entities, in order to disclose level of risk associated with new products; and
- the criteria used in the reward system at different management levels, including the board of directors.

4) Define and regulate eventual conflicts of interest in financial entities operating actively with customers in investment banking and commercial banking.
5) Avoid identifying 'better regulation' with higher government intervention in the day-to-day operations of financial entities.
6) Avoid undermining possible competitive advantages, discouraging financial innovation and fair risk taking. By discouraging innovation we may be limiting one source of economic growth.

Good practices of crisis management are crucial in order to start solving the problems. These practices are both *ex ante* and *ex post*. In any case, effective regulation and control of financial markets by financial authorities will imply a good understanding of the activities to be regulated, including some degrees of flexibility, realism and imagination.

8.6 Summary

Let's summarize the main points of this chapter.

1) The quality of a proposed restructuring can be analysed in terms of the following points:
   - Fairness
   - Stability
   - Company viability
   - Company value generation opportunities.
2) In order to be permanent, a restructuring agreement must be fair. The negotiations should produce agreements resulting in win–win solutions for all the parties involved.
3) The expected evolution of the company should be sustainable, based on realistic assumptions. How should we know when the assumptions are realistic? By being specific in identifying who will do what, when, how and through what means.
4) The best way to analyse the economic feasibility of a company is to understand clearly the amount and composition of the Net Cash Flow (NCF) it generates.
5) The quality of any restructuring process depends on how the business plan captures and reflects the key value drivers of the company, pointing

out its future opportunities and adapting the company to reach its objectives accordingly, not only in its operational aspects but in its future capital structure as well.

Appendices

Appendix 8.1

According to the assumptions of the business plan, the evolution of Publications, Inc. will be following (figures in thousand euros):

Evolution of Business Plan

Years	2014	2015	2016	2017	2018
Revenues	11,182	11,517	11,920	12,397	12,955
EBIT	224	288	358	434	518
Taxes on EBIT	56	65	72	87	104
EBIaT	168	223	286	347	415
Depreciation	337	347	359	373	390
FCL from P and L	505	570	645	721	805
FCL from Operating WC	–20	75	75	76	79
FCL from Capex	–500	–500	–500	–500	–500
Total FCF	–15	145	220	297	384

Years	2013	2014	2015	2016	2017	2018
Net Current Assets	1,322	1,342	1,267	1,192	1,116	1,036
Net Fixed Assets	5,058	5,221	5,374	5,515	5,642	5,752
Total Net Assets	6,380	6,563	6,641	6,707	6,758	6,788
Long-term Debt	3,406	3,406	3,406	3,406	3,406	3,406
Short-term Debt	851	994	986	906	748	496
Total Debt	4,257	4,400	4,392	4,312	4,153	3,902
EQUITY	2,123	2,163	2,250	2,395	2,604	2,886
Total D + E	6,380	6,563	6,641	6,707	6,758	6,788

Appendix 8.2

The valuation of Publications, Inc. associated with the business plan, considering a TV of 8.5 times E/EBITDA will be the following:

Years	2013	2014	2015	2016	2017	2018
E	5,939	6,268	6,615	6,978	7,359	7,720
D	4,257	4,400	4,392	4,312	4,153	3,902
V	10,196	10,668	11,006	11,290	11,512	11,622
Kd		4.00%	4.00%	4.00%	4.00%	4.00%
Kd (1–t)		3.00%	3.10%	3.20%	3.20%	3.20%
Rf		2.50%	2.50%	2.50%	2.50%	2.50%
MP		3.00%	3.00%	3.00%	3.00%	3.00%
Ke,u	4.90%	4.90%	4.90%	4.90%	4.90%	4.90%
Ke,l		5.55%	5.53%	5.50%	5.46%	4.90%
WACC		4.48%	4.53%	4.58%	4.59%	4.29%
FCF		–15	145	220	297	384
TV						11,622
FCF to discount		–15	145	220	297	12,006
Discount Factor		1.045	1.092	1.142	1.195	1.246
FCF at PV		–15	133	193	248	9,637
EV	10,196					

Note that we assume a cost of debt of 4.0%, a Market Premium of 3.0% and a Risk Free of 2.5%. The unleveraged beta of Publications, Inc. is estimated as 0.8.

This Terminal Value (TV) of 10,196 for EV is 14.1 times the EBITDA in 2018. The associated TV for E is 8.5 times the EBITDA of 2018.

In terms of an extrapolation of the last FCF, TV of EV is equal to the Present Value (PV) of a perpetuation of the FCF for 2018, growing at 0.95% and forever.

9
Summary and Conclusions

From Chapter 1

1) Over the last few years, the continuity of a large number of companies has depended at some time on a debt restructuring process to which the senior management of the firms in question have dedicated a considerable amount of effort and time. In short, companies in highly diverse sectors have survived – or gone under – as a result of their capacity to restructure and refinance their debts.
2) A company needs a restructuring process when it is facing a situation of economic distress. A company is in a situation of economic distress when it does not generate enough cash flow to cover the payments required by its debt with financial entities.
3) Of course, this lack of cash to cover payments of the service of debt must be a permanent situation, since any temporary imbalance might be covered with money coming from the shareholders.
4) Restructuring a company means introducing changes to a company to make it viable and profitable, given that the company is currently unfeasible and unprofitable. Although any corporate restructuring implies financial restructuring, it doesn't necessarily need to be only about its refinancing. The objective of any restructuring is to implement changes in the company so that it will generate enough FCF to cover the service of debt and remunerate its shareholders satisfactorily.
5) A restructuring process is a process of negotiation. As in all negotiating processes it is important to understand the interests of all the parties involved, recognizing their strong points and weak points, their negotiating clout, and so on.

   And, of course, it is important to know the answers to key questions, like:

Why did it happen?
What are the main debt restructuring actions that need to be taken?
What advantages will the debt restructuring process bring to the different parties involved?
What can the company offer to reach agreements in which everybody gains?

6) The key to success in any restructuring process is to reach an agreement whereby the value of the restructured company is greater than it would be if it were wound down, and then to agree on how this greater value should be distributed. One of the most important points for discussion is that of agreeing on a realistic plan for the future, and ensuring that securing sufficient free cash flow for short-term viability does not jeopardize the firm's medium- and long-term future by limiting investment plans that are essential for the continuity of the business.

From Chapter 2

1) Corporate financial restructuring involves activities both inside and outside the company. These actions taken within the company basically comprise:
   - Defining the liquidity problem: why, how much and when.
   - Preparing an internal financial plan, including a short-term treasury plan and a plan for medium- and long-term profitability.
   - Strategy for negotiations with the group of banks: what do we offer, to whom and under what conditions?
   - Preliminary proposal to put to the group of financial institutions.
2) The external actions involved in a financial restructuring process are aimed at achieving agreements between the parties, by identifying negotiators and possible arbiters, appointing experts for technical and legal matters, and establishing monitoring mechanisms so as to ensure compliance with the agreements.
3) As these external actions are carried out involving the banks, it is worth distinguishing between external actions with the banks' commercial area and external actions with their technical area.

From Chapter 3

1) The objective of any operating restructuring process is to implement operational actions in order to generate a sustainable increase in the Free Cash Flow (FCF). Although we can think about several managerial actions

that might temporarily increase the amount of cash, in a restructuring process we should look for a sustainable (permanent) effect. Restructuring is not about a short-term outlook, but a long-term one.

2) An operating restructuring focused on the generation of new and permanent FCF from operations will try to implement new policies and managerial decisions in relation to the different elements of the Profit and Loss of the company. Most operational managers are familiar with this kind of management – that we can call *management through P&L* – focused on fixing elements of the P&L: increase of Revenues, control of Operating Costs, reduction of General Expenses, etc.
3) An operating restructuring focused on the generation of new and permanent FCF from operating working capital should first of all be concerned with minimizing the current assets needed to meet the company's objectives, and thus only finance those resources that are strictly necessary. Working Capital Management certainly does not have the glamour of the company's other activities. But application of best practices on this issue can generate a sustainable flow of wealth. As always, the difference is in the details.
4) To estimate the profitability of a customer any company needs to estimate the real money that customer is generating to the company. From a financial perspective, a good customer is one that generates sustainable and sufficient cash flow to contribute to the feasibility and profitability of the company. In other words, a good customer is not only a customer that generates a good gross margin, but enough cash flow.
5) From an economic value perspective, all fixed assets should be classified into those that generate value, and those that don't. Keeping this in mind, in any restructuring process all fixed assets should be analysed from this point of view.
6) As a final remark, any operational restructuring requires analysis, decisions and management to implement them. Obviously, as in all management tasks, there is always the alternative of doing nothing. However, this is still a decision that leads to a form of management. And experience shows that this decision and this style of management are not favourable to the creation of value in the business.

From Chapter 4

1) Any company dealing with a corporate restructuring process has a lot of problems. To solve them it's necessary to understand their nature and causes. Most problems in a company come from the operating aspects, not

from the financial ones. Consequently, before trying to set up a permanent financial solution for a company, we need to understand why the company is not generating enough cash and we have to conceive a realistic and practicable business plan to address the critical issues. In other words, before trying to finance an operational problem, try to solve it. Financing operating inefficiencies is the best way to end in financial distress.

2) Financial leverage properly managed is a way to generate economic profitability in a company. Good management entails maintaining the level of debt within certain limits. In this context, one necessary step in any financial restructuring is to determine the debt capacity of the company.
3) When a company is involved in a corporate restructuring, to determine the debt capacity of that company we need to have a reference on the optimal capital structure the company should have.
4) Having decided the amount of debt and the capital structure associated to the financial restructuring, an additional important point is to select the type of debt to be used.
5) On this topic, there are some golden rules, like the following:
    - Finance short-term needs with short-term financing instruments, and long-term needs with long-term financing instruments.
    - Synchronize the timing on the service of the debt with the timing of the expected FCF.
    - Use the most appropriate debt instrument.
6) If a company does have operating problems, making changes only in financing is never the solution to them. Before operating problems, we need operating solutions, not *magical* financial solutions. But the situation can become even worse if the management of the troubled company makes errors in the financing.

    One of these errors can be trying to take advantage of the lack of symmetric information on the company among its different stakeholders. Lack of transparency is never a good policy.

From Chapter 5

1) In crisis situations gauging the economic value of a company's assets plays a key role in deciding whether to persevere with a business or not.
2) A company is considered to be in distress when it is unable to meet debt payments, often following failed attempts to generate the necessary cash flow by implementing operational restructuring measures.
3) In order to reach a debt restructuring agreement through a private procedure it is first necessary to do a valuation of the company.

4) It is therefore a question of agreeing on a valuation in which the banks accept that they would be better off being creditors of the restructured firm (the value of their stake being the debt) than being creditors of a company that is not going to be restructured (i.e. the liquidation value of the firm).
5) The key to carrying out a reasonable valuation lies in establishing the main objectives that the valuation process needs to achieve. This is particularly important in determining a reasonable value for a company in a situation of economic distress.
6) The economic value of the company in liquidation will obviously be the value it can obtain from the sale of all its net assets after tax. It is therefore a market value from which the applicable tax must be deducted.
7) To estimate the value of the restructured company it is necessary to estimate the Free Cash Flows (FCF) which would result from managing operating assets if the restructuring plan were to go ahead, and then discount these flows from the weighted average cost of capital (WACC) associated with these FCF and the new capital structure defined during the restructuring process.
8) This method produces an estimated value of the company's operating assets. If the company in distress has non-operating assets and the operating restructuring plan doesn't make provisions for their use, it will be necessary to make the pertinent adjustments (positive and negative) in order to include the value that could be derived from said operating assets.
9) Providing that with this restructuring the company will be economically feasible, the next step is to determine the expected economic profitability for the shareholders which will depend on the total value of the company and the value of its participation in the Equity.
10) The different scenarios that can be used in the negotiation process help to understand how difficult it might be to reach a fair balance among the participants in a restructuring process, in order to properly share the sacrifices needed to save the company.
11) In any case, we have to consider economic profitability (IRR of expected FCF for shareholders), not accounting profitability (average ROE).

From Chapter 8

1) The quality of a proposed restructuring can be analysed in terms of the following points:
    - Fairness
    - Stability

  - Company viability
  - Company value generation opportunities.
2) In order to be permanent, a restructuring agreement must be fair. The negotiations should produce agreements resulting in win–win solutions for all the parties involved.
3) The expected evolution of the company should be sustainable, based on realistic assumptions. How can we know when the assumptions are realistic? By being specific in identifying who will do what, when, how and through what means.
4) The best way to analyse the economic feasibility of a company is to understand clearly the amount and composition of the Net Cash Flow (NCF) it generates.
5) The quality of any restructuring process depends on how the business plan captures and reflects the key value drivers of the company, pointing out its future opportunities and adapting the company to reach its objectives accordingly, not only in its operational aspects but in its future capital structure as well.

Notes

1 Restructuring: A General Overview

1. Defined as ROE (ROE = Net Earnings/Equity).
2. For a more in-depth analysis of internal and external actions, see Francisco J. López Lubián (2010), 'Some Comments on Financial Restructuring', *Harvard Deusto Finanzas y Contabilidad*, December.

3 Operating Restructuring

1. See, for example, some classic book like Tom Peters (1999), *The Circle of Innovation*, Vintage Books).
2. See www.cfo.com.
3. Assuming two years of remaining depreciation (€ 250,000 per year) and a discount rate of 10%, the PV of tax savings associated with the differential depreciation would be € 130,165, at a tax rate of 30%.

4 Financial Restructuring

1. Proposition I in Modigliani and Miller (1954) concludes that the value of the company is independent of its capital structure and therefore separates investment and financing decisions based upon no arbitrage arguments and the absence of transaction costs (including taxes).
2. Although absurd business practices do sometimes occur, this is not usually very common. This is consistent with Modigliani–Miller Proposition II which provides a linear relationship between the cost of the unlevered assets, financial leverage and cost of risky debt under the assumption of absence of leverage or bankruptcy costs.
3. It is well known that passengers of airlines in financial difficulties always wonder if the aircraft are being properly maintained. This kind of mistrust can have a significant impact on the revenues of the businesses affected.
4. This is the so-called 'pecking order theory' arising under conditions of information asymmetry.
5. Examples of indirect costs of bankruptcy are shorter supplier payment deadlines during times of financial crisis, the inability to meet service commitments to customers, a drop in revenues due to managers' time being devoted to internal issues, etc. Examples of direct costs include legal costs, payments the company has to make to consultants advising on the bankruptcy process, etc.
6. This is one of the main reasons why business projects with a high level of initial leverage, such as project finance, leveraged buyouts (LBOs) or management buyouts (MBOs), have been carried out. To the extent that the operating risk is relatively

low and remains constant, with proper management of the risks affecting free cash flow, the project allows a greater degree of financial risk and generates more economic value, as the costs of debt do not rocket.

7. There are different ways to estimate these bankruptcy costs. Some authors use the formula:

   bc = probability of bankruptcy × cost of bankruptcy.

   The probability of bankruptcy can be approximated using a synthetic rating estimated for the company, based on historical data for the percentage of companies with a similar debt rating that went bankrupt over a given period of time. The cost of bankruptcy can also be estimated based on various studies published on the subject. As an indication, it is possible to talk of 5% of direct costs and up to 15% including indirect costs, according to various studies basing estimates on proxy variables. Appendix 4.1 includes a list of main bibliographical references in relation to the optimal capital structure.
8. In order to generate cash flow, it was essential to catalogue, value and sell off Cortefiel's real-estate assets as quickly as possible. Although the company's managers believed these assets to be worth around 300 million Euros, a recent independent valuation situated the value of this real estate at 150 million Euros. They expected to materialize the sale at the end of the first year.

5 Valuation in Distress

1. Total net assets are considered to be the sum of net current assets and net fixed assets. Net current assets are equivalent to the operating working capital, excluding short-term debt.
2. Also known as relative value or market value.
3. Also known as fundamental value.
4. In many cases it might be useful also to discount equity cash flows including in the cash flow calculations the details of all operating and financial restructuring measures. Cash flow to equity holders will show if the company is viable and profitable if and when the restructuring has been implemented.
5. Equivalent to the present value of a perpetuity for the last FCF, growing at 3.5%.
6. Average ROE of the restructured company is 13%.

6 Some Examples of Restructuring (I)

1. Fiscal year ending in April.
2. Fábricas Agrupadas de Muñecas de Onil, Sociedad Anónima (FAMOSA).
3. For more information on the company's business, see the website http://www.famosa.es/.
4. According to the initial business plan, in the event of breach of this condition in any given year, a reserve fund would be set aside equal to the amount of cash flow necessary. This fund would be created with additional capital from shareholders.
5. These theoretical returns are based on the assumption of no legal restriction. This means that all the positive FCF to shareholders will be freely distributed, in the

form of dividends or any other way to compensate the shareholders (e.g. shares buy back, issue of free new capital, etc.). In Spain there was a legal restriction regarding maintaining a capital reserve ratio that had to be considered. According to this legal restriction, the accumulated losses must not be more than two thirds of the capital over two years. If this happens, the shareholders' FCF may not be freely distributed and will be modified by possible capital infusions to ensure the ratio is maintained. For more information, see: http://www.bde.es/webbde/es/estadis/infoest/a1901.pdf.

7 Some Examples of Restructuring (II)

1. Figures in A$ million.
2. See details in Appendix 7.1.
3. Similar to the PV of a perpetuation of the last FCF with no growth (g=0).
4. http://www.sabmiller.com.
5. http://www.businessweek.com/news/2011-03-29/sabmiller-s-mackay-predicts-further-beer-industry-consolidation.html.
6. http://www.brewersofeurope.org/docs/flipping_books/contribution_report_2011/index.html#/8/zoomed.
7. http://ezinearticles.com/?Beer-Industry-Analysis&id=2977137.
8. http://www.sabmiller.com/files/presentations/2011/210911/210911_fosters.pdf.
9. Note on the goodwill implied in the transaction (A$ 9.9bn–A$ 0.4bn = A$ 9.5bn): Foster's equity was negatively affected in 2011 to the amount of almost A$ 2.2bn due to the demerger of its wine business. In any case, the relevance of this goodwill relates to the capacity of Foster's business to generate enough cash flows to provide for a reasonable return for SABMiller's investment.

8 Life after Restructuring

1. Of course, in relative terms.
2. See Chapter 4.
3. Appendix 8.1 develops a detailed explanation of the expected future for the company, following the assumptions of the restructuring plan.
4. See Appendix 8.2 for details of the valuation.
5. Copeland, T., Koller, T. and Murrin, J. (2002) *Valuation*. John Wiley & Sons, Inc.
6. In fact, these paragraphs come from the Message of Pope Benedict XVI, called 'Fighting Poverty to Build Peace' and published for the celebration of the World Day of Peace (1 January 2009). I believe this is a very interesting document. And surprising (kind of...).

Index

Printed and bound by CPI Group (UK) Ltd, Croydon, CR0 4YY